Effective Teaching

with Internet Technologies

Effective Teaching

with Internet Technologies

Pedagogy and Practice

Alan Pritchard

P·C·P

Paul Chapman
Publishing

First published 2007

Paul Chapman Publishing
A SAGE Publications Company
1 Oliver's Yard
55 City Road
London EC1Y 1SP

SAGE Publications Inc
2455 Teller Road
Thousand Oaks, California 91320

SAGE Publications India Pvt Ltd
B 1/I 1 Mohan Cooperative Industrial Area
Mathura Road, Post Bag 7
New Delhi 110 044

SAGE Publications Asia-Pacific Pte Ltd
33 Pekin Street #02-01
Far East Square
Singapore 048763

Library of Congress Control Number: 2007921672

**A catalogue record for this book is available from
the British Library**

ISBN 978-1-4129-3094-9
ISBN 978-1-4129-3095-6 (pbk)

Typeset by C&M Digitals (P) Ltd., Chennai, India
Printed in Great Britain by Athenaeum Press, Gateshead, Tyne and Wear
Printed on paper from sustainable resources

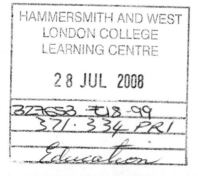

Dedication

This book is dedicated firstly to a large group of creative teachers for allowing me to share their ideas, secondly to Jackie, my wife, for allowing me to go missing so often, and lastly to my daughters, Maria and Frances, for allowing me occasional use of my computer. I love you all.

Contents

List of Figures

List of Tables

Acknowledgements

Thank you to all teachers and children who have let me observe and question at will. Without the access to classrooms and without the time that teachers have freely given over the last years this book would not have been possible.

Companion Website

You can find a companion website for this book at www.sagepub.co.uk/pritchard.
The site links you to related websites for most of the case studies, as well as featuring
images of children's work and other supporting material. There is also some suggested
reading that you might like to follow up, and extracts from some of the author's other
published work.

1 ICT, the Internet and Theories of Learning

About this chapter

In this chapter you will encounter:

- an explanation of the purpose and structure of the book
- a general review of learning theory as it might relate to the use of the internet
- a detailed consideration of constructivist learning theory with particular reference to the use of ICT and the internet.

INTRODUCTION

This book has been written with the intention of looking in detail at some of the issues surrounding the increasing use of the internet in schools. The book also looks at the associated areas of learning theory and pedagogy, which are likely to have an impact on the realisation of the expected learning outcomes that teachers formulate and work towards.

The book provides the background to learning theory relevant to a consideration of internet use in schools, and presents an overview of current views and developments concerning pedagogy in the light of the advent of new technologies in general, and the internet in particular.

To exemplify some of the important ideas and approaches considered in the early chapters of the book a series of case studies, grouped according to learning and pedagogical principles, is also included. The case studies serve to provide a strong practical input, helping to make the book useful for academics and practitioners alike. The case studies are based on classroom research and as such are examples of the sort of work currently being undertaken by teachers. The case studies emphasise the planning and practicalities of the work and links are made to the theory that is considered earlier in the book. The case studies also consider the learning outcomes and compare them, as far as this is possible, to the outcomes which might have been achieved if the work had been undertaken in a more traditional and non-ICT related way.

LEARNING THEORY AND THE USE OF ICT AND THE INTERNET

Naturally everything that teachers do in their planning and their teaching, as well as most of their interactions with their pupils, is centred on the idea that children learn in certain ways and that teachers plan and design activities to take advantage of this.

The arrival of new technologies in schools in the 1980s had little impact on the way that teachers planned and taught. Many computer applications that were used in classrooms were copies of approaches that teachers had used, and in some cases, had stopped using over the years. An example of this is the increase in the number of programs that gave extensive repetition in basic skills and became known as "drill and practice" programs. There is a place for this type of program perhaps, but to concentrate the power of a sophisticated and expensive piece of equipment on an outdated approach to learning with questionable value is not wholly satisfactory.

With the growing awareness of the theory associated with learning and a growing interest in the ways that new technologies might change the way that teachers teach and children learn, there is scope, perhaps even a real need, to look at what is currently known about learning, especially in relation to the new possibilities afforded by Information and Communications Technologies (ICTs).

If we deal quickly with the behaviourist view of learning, we will be able to concentrate on the constructivist theories, which seem to give far better representations of the complex processes involved in learning. Put simply, behaviourists see learning as a process by which learners become able to make specific set responses to particular stimuli. This perhaps sounds very basic, and in some ways it is, but behaviourists believe that all behaviour can be divided into small actions, each of which can be mastered by a process of training, rewards and sometimes punishments, and that learning proceeds in that way, often without the all important ingredient of understanding.

To be able to respond with the number 56 when asked the question "What are seven eights?" is certainly commendable. However, simply responding with the correct number cannot give any insight into the level of understanding of the respondent. Of course we can say that as long as the answer is correct it does not matter, but understanding is at the heart of effective and lasting learning. Some would argue that being able to make the correct response is fine and that understanding may follow on behind for many, and if it does not, then at least the response is correct.

In many contexts behaviourist style learning may be the answer, reciting multiplication tables may be one of these contexts, and there are others – automatically looking both ways before crossing a road; saying "please" and "thank you" appropriately; putting "i" before "e" except after "c". There are many more contexts when what is really needed is the flexibility that comes with understanding. Generally speaking we have moved away from behaviourist style teaching and learning for most learning activities, and the school of thought that holds sway, though not always explicitly, is the school of constructivist learning.

Constructivism, in contrast to earlier theories, puts understanding at a high level of priority. Constructivism, as the name suggests, sees learning as a building activity in which individuals build an understanding of events, concepts and processes, based on their personal experiences and often supported and developed by, amongst other things, activity and interaction with others.

Let us look at this in a little more detail. If we were to distil what has been written about constructivist learning we might come down to the following four statements.

- Learning is a process of interaction between what is known and what is to be learned.
- Learning is a social process.

- Learning is a situated process.
- Learning is a metacognitive process.

We will look at each of these in turn.

LEARNING AS A PROCESS OF INTERACTION BETWEEN WHAT IS KNOWN AND WHAT IS TO BE LEARNED

We all have a wealth of prior knowledge and understanding, which we can call upon and bring to bear on any new situation in which we find ourselves. This need not be a formal learning situation, it could be anything: problem solving, choosing a route, interpreting a coded message, but for this discussion let us think more about situations where learning is planned, and indeed, expected.

Whenever we begin a new learning topic in school we bring to it what we have already learned, our factual knowledge – sea water is "salty"; our understanding – energy is transferable and can be neither created nor destroyed; and our skills – the ability to multiply two-digit numbers together. We are also quite likely to bring to the new learning some misunderstandings, or "incorrect" facts – the sun travels around the Earth in space; swans are male ducks; steam and smoke are the same things.

The misunderstandings or incorrect facts exist for one reason or another. They may be misconstruction, they may be misinterpretations based on insufficient evidence. Whatever the reason for their existence, they exist in the same way as the facts and understandings that are more accurate exist, and they are the starting point for learning more about the given topic.

Constructivist theory tells us that we build new understanding upon existing understanding. In this way, whatever the starting point, learning will have taken place when something has been added – something new built upon what exists already. We can explain this better perhaps in terms of schema theory. We build mental models of the real world in order to help us to understand what we see, hear or otherwise experience. "Human beings understand the world by constructing models of it in their minds." (Johnson-Laird, 1983: 43) These mental models are sometimes referred to as "schemas".

Beginning with Piaget in the 1920s, followed by Bartlett (1930s), Schank (1970s) and Rumelhart (1980s), many psychologists have examined and developed the notion of schemas. Johnson-Laird (1983) suggests that mental models are the basic structure of human thought: "It is now plausible to suppose that mental models play a central and unifying role in representing objects, states of affairs, sequences of events, the way the world is, and the social and psychological actions of daily life." And Holland considers that "… mental models are the basis for all reasoning processes." (Holland et al., 1986: 194)

A schema can be thought of as a theoretical multi-dimensional store for many millions of items of knowledge. A schema is a framework with numerous nodes and even more numerous connections between nodes. At each node there is a discrete piece of information or an idea. The piece of information can be in any one of many different forms – an image, a sound, a smell, a feeling, an action, and more. Each node is connected to a great many others. The connections between nodes are made as a result of there being a semantic link between the connected items. The links are personal, and identical items in the schemas of two different people are very likely to have very different links made for very different reasons, which could account for individuals having a different perspective on and understanding of a topic. It is the mental process of adding new items to schemas, and forging connections between them and the existing framework, that constitutes constructivist learning.

As there is no limit to the size to which a schema might grow, there is also no limit to the number of connections within a schema: there are no restrictions on how schemas might link and interconnect with other schemas. The more connections there are within and between schemas, the more construction has taken place, and the more it is considered that knowledge and understanding has been gained, and learning has taken place.

Schemas can be characterised in the following ways.

- Schemas are based on our general world knowledge and experiences.
- Schemas are generalised knowledge about situations, objects, events, feelings and actions.
- Schemas are incomplete and constantly evolving.
- Schemas are personal.
- Schemas are not usually fully accurate representations of a phenomenon.
- Schemas often include inaccuracies and contradictions (misconceptions).
- Schemas provide simplified explanations of complex phenomena.
- Schemas often contain uncertainty but are used even if incorrect.
- Schemas guide our understanding of new information by providing explanations of what is happening, what it means and what is likely to result.

Prior knowledge has a crucial part to play in constructivist learning. An existing schema represents the sum of an individual's current state of knowledge and understanding of the topic in question. New learning concerned with the topic will involve the processes of assimilation (adding new information) and accommodation (adding new information and altering existing structures) and the expansion, and increase in complexity, of the schema in question. For this reason it is very important that a schema which is to be the focus of these processes in the introduction of a new area of work in school, is activated and revisited at the outset of a new topic, and re-activated in subsequent lessons. The starting point of what is already known and understood is very important if any new learning is to be effective. Schema activation is a process that can be encouraged in classroom situations, and teachers frequently make use of this idea in their work.

To summarise, psychologists refer to units of knowledge, understanding and skill as schemas. This is a way of referring to conceptual knowledge that is stored in long term memory. It is estimated that adults have hundreds of thousands of schemas in place, all of which are interrelated in an extremely large number of different ways. New schemas are regularly created and existing schemas are constantly updated. The process of creating and updating takes place every time that we read, listen to, observe, try out, or sense in any other way, anything new. New schemas are created every time one fact is linked to another by a logical or semantic connection. Each schema is a sub-schema of another larger and related schema, and each schema has a set of sub-schemas of its own.

Mayer (1983) sets out four elements that describe a schema.

- General: a schema may be used in a wide variety of situations as a framework for understanding incoming information.
- Knowledge: a schema exists in memory as something which a person knows.
- Structure: a schema is organised around a theme.
- Comprehension: a schema contains slots which are filled in by specific information.

LEARNING AS A SOCIAL PROCESS

Piaget, possibly the first constructivist, had a view of the growing child as a "lone scientist". This view depicts a child alone, exploring the immediate environment and drawing conclusions about the nature and structure of their world. Social constructivism gives us an important new dimension to the domain. Social constructivist theory emphasises interaction between the learner and others. The "other" can come in many forms – parent, peer, teacher, it is the dimension of social interaction that is crucial. The main proponents of this branch of constructivism are Lev Vygotsky, a Russian whose work was carried out at the start of the twentieth century, but not widely available in the West until many years later, and Jerome Bruner, an American working and publishing in the second half of the twentieth century.

Social constructivism gives a high priority to language in the process of intellectual development. Dialogue is considered to be the means by which ideas are considered, shared and shaped. Dialogue is often with a more knowledgeable other, but this need not always be the case as equally valuable in terms of social constructivism is dialogue with peers. Prior knowledge, naturally, has a part to play. It is an individual's prior and current knowledge that forms the basis of any contribution made to a dialogue, and it is with reference to existing knowledge and understanding (schemas) that new ideas and understanding can be constructed in the course of dialogue. The more knowledgeable other need not be a teacher, or a parent, and more knowledgeable need not imply older, or position of responsibility for learning.

Obviously learning is not restricted to the location of the classroom. Social interaction with anybody, at any time, and in any place may well lead to learning. The building and exchange of thoughts and ideas which takes place in the course of a discussion, in any context at all, is likely for at least one of the participants, to lead to a greater understanding of, or insight into, the topic in question.

In formal learning situations, such as classrooms, the role of the more knowledgeable other is most often taken by a teacher, though peer–peer dialogue is also very important. The teacher has the role of initiating dialogue and maintaining its momentum. In a very real way, the teacher engages pupils in dialogue and supports the development of understanding. The undertaking of this role, in a planned way, has a particular name: scaffolding. To fully understand the concept of scaffolding we need to first look at an aspect of Vygotsky's work, which is the notion of a zone of proximal development (ZPD).

The zone of proximal development is a refreshingly simple description of something that many teachers and other adults understand and work with, although they may not necessarily realise that they do. It is an aspect of Vygotsky's work which has made considerable impact on practice over recent years, particularly as greater importance has been given to the notion of classroom differentiation.

The zone of proximal development is a theoretical space of understanding that lies just above the level of an individual's current understanding. It is the next level of understanding that a learner is working towards. In the zone of proximal development a learner is only able to work effectively with support. The zone, necessarily, will be different for each individual at any given stage for any particular topic. In terms of this theoretical area of understanding the process of learning involves moving into and across the zone and looking towards the next level of understanding, which will involve making similar progress across a new zone of proximal development. Sewell (1990) describes the ZPD as "a point at which a child has partly mastered a skill but can act more effectively with the assistance of a more skilled adult or peer".

Making progress through the ZPD is a process that can be assisted by the intervention of another. In formal situations this intervention might be planned, but often a timely and, well judged intervention depends upon circumstances that cannot necessarily be predicted, and therefore depends on the progress made by the learner at a given time, and, in many situations, also upon the skill and experience of the teacher. In many cases a teacher will fulfil this role, but others are equally capable and likely to do so. In planning work for children a teacher needs to take into account the current state of the understanding of the children in question, and plan accordingly and appropriately. In an ideal situation this could mean planning for individuals, but in a more realistic situation this is not usually possible.

Scaffolding is the name given to the process of giving support to learners at the appropriate time, at the appropriate level of sophistication, and in an appropriate way to meet the individual's needs. Scaffolding takes place in many ways, some carefully planned – the provision of tailored materials for example, others in a more spontaneous way – a timely question, or reminder perhaps. So scaffolding can be through discussion – a good socially constructive approach, through the provision of materials – perhaps supplying practical apparatus to help in the solution of problems in arithmetic, or by designing tasks that match the level of understanding of the individual and provide appropriate help – a list of words given to help in the process of completing an exercise designed to assist understanding, or a list of reminders concerning the process of undertaking the task in question – a writing frame to support a particular style of writing piece is an example of this.

Working collaboratively with others, in pairs or small groups, is an obvious socially constructive approach to learning. There are times when quiet individual working is useful and important, but as a core approach this would ignore all that is known about learning that is socially constructed.

The role of the computer in general, and the internet in particular may not be immediately clear in the context of socially constructed learning. We will see later that there are times when the internet is used in a way that is not geared towards dialogue or collaboration, but there are times, which will also be exemplified, when the use of the internet can be clearly identified as a means of promoting this type of learning. For example:

- There are times when a dialogue, though perhaps not an oral dialogue, is encouraged, even required when interacting with particular software. Questions might need answers, or choices might be required. There are good examples of internet activities that encourage a level of interaction with the software, which can amount to the sort of dialogue likely to encourage thought and understanding.

- In a more realistic, though sometimes less immediate way, dialogue can be undertaken by means of electronic communication. We will see that this might be in what is known as "real time" communication (synchronous), often referred to as "chat", or asynchronous, such as e-mail exchanges which continue over a longer period of time, involving time delays with responses.
- Also, activities mediated by the internet can be a stimulus for dialogue between those taking part, either at the time, or at a later time away from the computer.

In this more recognisable way, computer and internet use can promote and inspire dialogue between users. When children are asked to work in pairs or small groups, the reason is often to allow them to discuss ideas related to the work and to work together towards a shared end product. The particular activity deriving from the internet is a stimulus for generating talk at the computer, and even when away from the computer, in work related to the task in hand. This aspect of computer use has been investigated in depth by researchers such as Mercer (1994), Phillips (1990) and also Fisher (1996).

LEARNING AS A SITUATED PROCESS

Situated learning refers to the fact that all learning takes place in a context – learning cannot take place in a "content vacuum". The context may, or may not, be one which is familiar to the learner. The importance of this notion is in the belief that if the context is unfamiliar to the learner, learning will not necessarily proceed smoothly.

Situated learning (Lave and Wenger, 1991) suggests that skills, knowledge and understanding that are learned in one context may not necessarily be transferred successfully to another. Another aspect of situated learning, which is probably more relevant here, is the notion that learning is most often situated in social and cultural settings, and that if a learning context falls beyond the cultural understanding of the learner then learning is likely, at best, to be less successful than if had it been located in a more familiar setting. For example, asking children from a socially deprived area to devise and solve maths problems related to expensive holidays, currency exchange and air travel might not be appropriate (it might actually be considered highly insensitive). In the same way it would be difficult for children from a remote rural area to understand and work in a context that is steeped in the mores and conventions of an inner city area with high proportions of ethnic minority inhabitants.

There is a link between the idea of learning being situated, and the need for learning to be in some way authentic. We are told that authentic tasks are: "… tasks which children can relate to their own experience inside the classroom; tasks which an experienced practitioner would undertake." (Selinger, 2001: 96) When learning is made up of authentic tasks there is a greater probability of engagement with the task and also with the information and ideas involved. Authentic tasks are likely to hold the attention and interest of learners and lead to a deeper level of engagement than with another similar but "non-authentic" or possibly "less authentic" task. This links closely with the ideas put forward by the socio-cultural learning theorists. Bruner (1996), Brown et al. (1989) and others support the need for culturally linked and authentic learning tasks, this has the desirable effect of making the difference between learning in school and "out of school learning" less well defined. Children working with new ideas in a context that they recognise and to which they can easily relate, are far more likely to take an interest, and to engage with the ideas than if the same ideas are presented in a context alien to them.

In one sense, the internet provides a vehicle, if not a context, for learning which, for many learners, is familiar. This, on its own, is not a strong argument in favour of internet use, but it is a contributory factor. The way that the internet can give context to school work is in the provision of examples: settings which are culturally recognisable, possibly in the guise of stories, locations, maps, products and popular cultural artefacts. The internet can also provide authenticity by presenting real places, real statistics, real events, real people to communicate with and real problems for consideration. Much of this – context and authenticity – may well have been available before the advent of the internet, but never has it been so easily accessible and so freely available.

LEARNING AS A METACOGNITIVE PROCESS

Metacognition refers to the idea of an individual considering, being aware of, and otherwise understanding their own mental (cognitive) processes and ways of learning. Cognition is an overall term that includes all of the mental activities that facilitate the acquisition, storage, retrieval and use of knowledge. Cognition also refers to the ability to think, to process and store information, and to solve problems; it is considered to be a high level behaviour that may be unique to humans. Obviously the role of cognition in the process of learning is crucial. Metacognition can be thought of as cognition relating to cognition – it is an individual's awareness of their own thought processes. This awareness can make a difference, sometimes a profound difference, to the way that individuals view their own learning. An awareness of one's own thought and learning processes is likely, with encouragement, to lead to a recognition of the ways in which personal learning might proceed effectively.

We can define metacognitive knowledge as the knowledge that an individual has about their own cognition, which can be used to consider and to control their cognitive processes. To be metacognitively aware, and to work metacognitively, is to consider and take control of the processes involved in learning and thinking as they are happening.

John Flavell (1976, 1977) first made use of the term "metacognition". He tells us that metacognition consists of metacognitive knowledge and metacognitive experiences or regulation. Metacognitive knowledge is knowledge about cognitive processes, which an individual has come to understand, and can be used to control mental processes: "Metacognition refers to one's knowledge concerning one's cognitive processes and products or anything related to them ... metacognition refers, among other things, to the active monitoring ... regulation and orchestration of these processes." (Flavell, 1976) Brown (1987) offers a simpler version of this when he says that

"Metacognition refers loosely to one's knowledge and control of his/her own cognitive system".

An example of when some small measure of metacognitive understanding can be of benefit might be when a "learning" task is set, possibly for homework. For some learners, to be told "Learn this for homework", might be as helpful as asking them to learn to fly to school. They are likely, in some cases, to have absolutely no idea about how to go about doing it. They might resort to staring at words on a page, if they bother to try anything at all. Others might have an idea of how to approach a task of this type. They will have, although they would not express it in this way, some personal metacognitive knowledge. They will have devised techniques for learning – reading, writing, note-taking, closing their eyes and recalling, even the social option of asking someone to help, by way of a test of some sort. Whatever they are able to do in order to help them learn is an example of cognitive activity of some sort or another being actively controlled.

Children are, at times, completely lost when it comes to undertaking simple mental calculation. Individual approaches to mental calculation vary widely and some approaches seem complicated and difficult to one person and clear and simple to another. The Cockcroft Report (DES, 1982) found that the ways in which adults undertook mental arithmetic tasks varied enormously and that idiosyncratic approaches were widespread. This is wholly acceptable if arriving at the correct answer is the prime objective, but for young children trying to find their way with mental calculation, insight into their own approaches and processes can be important. This insight into how to think, in what are for some complex abstract terms, is metacognitive, and very helpful in the process of learning how to undertake the task in question.

Teachers encourage approaches to the development of metacognitive awareness in simple ways. Children can be asked to describe their own approaches, and by giving value to the identification of the methods and processes followed by different individuals, awareness of different ways of thinking and working can be encouraged. Instead of being satisfied with a correct answer, a teacher can probe and discover the approach taken. Teachers and children alike can begin to note when a method is valid, even if an incorrect answer is arrived at.

The process of sharing and experimenting with different approaches to carrying out mental calculations in an environment which is safe and supportive can, in a socially constructive way, lead to individuals developing both a fuller understanding of their own processes of thinking, and in this case, an understanding of how to tackle particular tasks that they might previously have considered too difficult for them to attempt.

A consideration of which approaches best suit an individual can be of immense value at times of "routine" learning – such times as when learning spellings, practising methods in maths, or other factual content which needs to be internalised; it can be useful at times when revision is undertaken for exams. However, there is more to metacognitive approaches than devising ways of memorising.

Metacognition, when applied in general learning situations might imply asking the children to consider what they are doing, how they are approaching their work, how they intend to use the information that they have found to meet the requirements of the task they are undertaking – how they are working out solutions to numerical problems; how they deal with the responses of others, particularly if they contradict something which they believe to be true. Some strategies might be provided for them to experiment with, but it must be remembered that one strategy might be ideally suitable for one learner, and of no real use to another.

There are metacognitive strategies that can be of value in computer and internet-related situations. The ideas above apply equally in situations involving computer use and the use of the internet. Metacognitive thinkers will make decisions based upon their knowledge of their own preferences and learning inclinations, which will guide how they use resources found on the internet. They will know, for example, that it is not going to be helpful, at least in their case and in terms of developing understanding, to simply copy and paste text from a website to a piece of their own work. (There will be some who see this as a satisfactory approach.) They might know, for example, that if they are to benefit from the exercise they will need to print the text and mark it up with a highlighter pen, drawing attention, for their own benefit, to the important points in the text. For another this technique would not be suitable, and they would have another means of engaging with the content of the text. It is possible for teachers to draw attention to metacognitive concerns and to encourage learners to think in ways that will help them to understand their own cognition and benefit from this knowledge when they engage in learning activities.

There are several types of internet based activity which, when introduced with the development of metacognitive thinking in mind, can assist in the process of solving problems and with learning in general. Problem-solving activities of different types, mathematical/logical activities and some learning/revision activities all have the potential to increase a child's understanding of their own cognitive processes and learning preferences. There is a connection between the skills and knowledge involved in formulating effective searches with internet search engines and thinking logically and, in a sense, metacognitively. Teaching search techniques, possibly in the context of other content based work, is a valuable undertaking as, firstly, it can make the child a more effective user of the internet and, secondly, the understanding required for formulating effective searches is transferable to other areas of work and is related to other metacognitive strategies.

Finally on the matter of constructivist learning, we can look at a set of important features that constructivist learning theory seems to be built around, and which are summed-up below under headings proposed by Jonassen et al. (1999).

Knowledge construction and not knowledge reproduction is paramount

It is the processes that the learner puts into place and uses that are important for the construction of new knowledge and understanding, rather than the fact of knowing something as an end product. A learner is actively engaged and in control of the learning process.

Authentic tasks in a meaningful context are encouraged

Authentic tasks, such as problem-solving, are used to situate learning in familiar, interesting and realistic contexts.

Reflection on prior experience is encouraged

Learners are prompted to relate new knowledge and concepts to pre-existing knowledge and experience, which allows the "new" to integrate with what is already known.

Collaborative work for learning is encouraged

Dialogue with others allows additional and alternative perspectives to be taken into account when developing personal conclusions. Different knowledge, points of view, and understanding can be taken and considered before moving on.

Autonomy in learning is encouraged

Learners are given and accept increasing amounts of responsibility for their own learning. This happens in a number of different ways – by collaborating with others, by working on self generated problems, and by the forming and testing of hypotheses, for example.

From what we know about constructivism and about pedagogy it might be reasonable to consider that a pedagogy that emphasises communication in its widest sense, and also encourages communal, collaborative and cooperative work that leads to the joint construction of new knowledge and understanding is something which teachers should be encouraged to develop. Indeed, many teachers do use this approach, to some extent or another. A pedagogy that embraces social constructivism and, with the help of internet-based technologies, takes it further and develops the use of information and the scope for social interaction that would not in other ways be easily accessible is a positive, theory based and practically tested approach to teaching, which can be promoted in classrooms in the knowledge that it is a sound and potentially successful approach. This is not to say that all other pedagogies reliant on other theoretical standpoints should be banished. We will see later that there are good examples of effective learning that are predicated on, for example, lone working and semi-behaviourist principles. In these examples, however, the introduction of basic metacognitive thought, the encouragement of a small measure of discussion and the recognition by teachers that the work might be further improved in a variety of ways related to social constructivist ideas point to the probable value of a varied approach to pedagogy, though with a strong emphasis on what is known about constructivism. One point that has been raised over the years is that teachers seem to be more effective when working in ways which, in some way, suit them. That is, teachers who are experienced in and comfortable with a particular way of working tend to be more successful than when they use an approach that they do not have experience of and do not feel comfortable with. This is in no way an argument for a no change scenario, but it must be remembered that in some cases teachers need to gain experience of new approaches gradually, and an approach to teaching that encompasses a variety of approaches and pedagogies is not altogether a bad thing.

SUMMARY

The internet is becoming an important resource for use in schools and as such it has created the need to look again at what we know about how children learn, and about how teachers approach the tasks involved in teaching.

Of all of the websites that might be used for teaching purposes, some are specifically designed for schools and include activities and tasks to complete, others can be equally useful but have not been created with educational purposes as a priority. The tasks and other activities presented on websites, and the ways in which teachers choose to encourage children to make use of websites, is underpinned by certain theoretical approaches to teaching and learning. Sometimes the theory has affected the design of the site, sometimes the approach chosen by the teacher dictates the type and style of learning that is encouraged. Teachers need to be aware of the underpinning theory, which can have a big effect on the progress of learning. Teachers need to have clear learning outcomes in mind, and according to these, plan appropriately. Sometimes a behaviourist approach may be most appropriate, at other times an approach based upon constructivist principles may be.

Behaviourist learning, sometimes characterised by memorising, or rote learning, does not necessarily lead to an understanding of ideas, but can be quite effective for encouraging recall of facts. Constructivist learning involves more thinking, more activity, and more interaction with others. Constructivist learning encourages and implies understanding.

The principles of constructivist learning, which in many cases are the most appropriate to apply in learning situations (whether or not the internet is implicated) are:

- learning is a process of interaction between what is known and what is to be learned
- learning is a social process
- learning is a situated process
- learning is a metacognitive process.

2 The Internet, Pedagogy and Learning

About this chapter

In this chapter you will encounter:

- background to the use of the internet in schools
- the importance of evaluating internet resources
- a discussion of the key features of ICT as they relate to learning
- an overview and discussion of different pedagogies as they relate to the use of ICT and the internet
- reference to the essential links between pedagogy and learning theory
- characteristics of constructivist learning, which might be present in effective ICT related lessons.

NATURE AND HISTORY OF THE INTERNET IN SCHOOLS

The national curriculum for schools in England (DfEE/QCA, 1999) sets out four strands which, when combined, make up the notional subject of ICT. The word "notional" is used here because there is a strong emphasis placed on the use of ICT as a means of supporting learning in subjects, rather than ICT for its own end. There is a debate in academic circles concerning the nature of ICT as a subject, but this will not be discussed here. (See Hammond, 2004, Webb, 2002, Somekh, 2000, Cordes and Miller, 2000)

The four strands are:

- finding things out
- developing ideas and making things happen
- exchanging and sharing information
- reviewing, modifying and evaluating work as it progresses.

Traditionally, insofar as there is a tradition concerning the use of the internet in schools, it is the first strand of the national curriculum for ICT – finding things out, that has been the focus of internet use. There have been, however, many developments that allow the internet to support all of the strands.

When Tim Berners-Lee (Berners-Lee, in Dern, 1994: 73), sometimes referred to as the inventor of the internet (even though no one person can be considered to be individually responsible), described the result of his supposed invention as a, "... wide-area hypermedia information retrieval initiative aiming to give universal access to a large universe of documents", he described the mysterious nature of something that many of us take for granted. The different elements of his definition are considered below.

Wide-area: The World Wide Web spans the entire globe.

Hypermedia: It contains a range of media, including text, pictures, sound and video. The individual elements are connected by hyperlinks that connect pages to one another, and allow for swift movement from one internet location to another.

Information retrieval: Viewing a web document is very easy thanks to the help of web browsers, which are the point of contact between the user and the web. Web browsers allow the user to retrieve pages just by clicking a mouse button when the pointer on the screen is over a "link", or by entering appropriate web addresses. Information may be retrieved from the web extremely quickly by any suitably set up computer with an internet connection.

Universal access: No matter what type of computer, or what type of computer the page that is to be viewed is stored on, web browsers allow for apparently seamless connection to and movement between many different internet locations which might be stored on many different types of computer system. Increasingly newer mobile devices, including mobile phones, are adding to this universal access.

Large universe of documents: Anyone can publish a web page. No matter what obscure information you want to find, there is certain to be someone who has produced and published a web page about it. It will not necessarily be exactly what you want, it might not be accurate or written in an appropriate style, but it will be there. "The Net consists of 2.5 billion documents, growing at a healthy clip of 7.3 million pages per day." (Varian, undated)

INTERNET USE IN SCHOOLS

The internet, by means of the World Wide Web, and initially by the use of simple e-mail systems, has become the latest in a list of technological advances to be introduced into classrooms. In the early to mid 1990s to use the internet in a primary school setting was to take a bold move into the unknown. (Only 17 per cent of primary schools even had access to the internet by 1998, see below.) At first access was slow and unreliable and the internet was only a tool for the enthusiasts. To make use of the internet in school was not a particularly obvious option to follow. Certainly information of one sort or another could be sought out for use in lessons, but to rely on the system, which was an expensive undertaking apart from anything else, to provide access for the duration of a lesson, was asking too much. The use of e-mail was introduced experimentally, and in some schools contact was made, sometimes only locally, with other classes. Examples of contact between more remote locations at home and abroad soon came to light. As the availability and reliability of the equipment increased, so did the opportunities for teachers to try out new communications-based activities.

Official figures from the UK Government give a picture of the current position as far as schools with internet access is concerned: since 2002 more than 99 per cent of

Table 2.1 **Percentage of schools connected to the internet since 19** (Source: DfES 2004a)

Year	Percentage of schools connected to th						
	1998	1999	2000	2001	2002		
Primary	17	62	86	96	>99		
Secondary	83	93	98	>99	>99	>	>99
Special	31	60	92	97	>99	>9	>99
All schools	28	66	88	97	>99	>99	>99

all schools have had access to the internet. This is not a wholly foolproof measure of internet use because it gives no indication of the use to which the internet connection is put, or whether the connection is used at all. However, it does show an incredible increase over the preceding few years.

Despite the rapid increase in internet connectivity in schools, it is important to remember that, "The internet is a generally unregulated environment ..." and, "There is a wide range of material available covering virtually every aspect of our life or activity, much of it positive, some of it offensive." (DfES, undated) As well as being very large and generally of a positive nature, another aspect of the make up of the internet that must be held firmly in mind is that a very large proportion of the internet is attempting to sell to the sometimes unsuspecting surfer.

Through access to the internet it is possible for children to "visit" places and take part in events that would otherwise be too far away, too dangerous, or too costly. For example, the 24 Hour Museum (www.24hourmuseum.org.uk) enables visitors to take a virtual tour, the Hubble Space Telescope (http://hubblesite.org or http://hubble.nasa.gov) offers full-colour pictures of planets, while the Whole Brain Atlas (www.med.harvard.edu/AANLIB/home.html) gives access to full colour MRI scan images of the entire brain. Video-conferencing allows for real time communication with experts. There are other sites specifically designed to support education in the UK, which offer pupils, teachers and parents access to a growing collection of good quality, "approved" resources and educational material. Searching for information on the Web can help pupils to develop information handling skills. The internet is an ideal vehicle for introducing pupils to, and illustrating, concepts such as audience, purpose, authorship and bias. By viewing sites that promote opposing views, the idea of subjectivity/objectivity, fact/opinion and overt/covert bias can be demonstrated in an immediate and powerful way. The internet is also a place for children to publish their own work.

WEBSITE EVALUATION

When any particular resource is chosen for use in a planned learning activity the teacher, either formally, or more likely, informally, will have made judgements about its usefulness. This process of evaluation becomes very important when dealing with a "large universe of documents". Teachers must be absolutely certain, for example, at information or activities accessed via the internet are wholly appropriate and in no way damaging or misleading.

The site Superhighway Safety formerly hosted by the Department for Education and Skills (DfES, undated) offered a list of website attributes that should be considered when making an evaluation of a web-based resource. Not all of the attributes will be relevant for every site, but the list makes a useful yardstick against which sites might be measured. The list of attributes is set out and discussed below.

- Authority
- Purpose
- Audience
- Relevance
- Objectivity
- Accuracy
- Currency
- Format
- Links
- Ease of use

These attributes are elaborated below (the attribute "Ease of use" has been added). Different sets of questions are presented here and can be asked in order to establish more information about a particular site, and to enable evaluations to be made based on more than initial impressions. Some of the questions are taken from the same source.

Authority

Who has written the information?
What is the authority or expertise of the author?
Are there contact details for the author?
From where does the content originate?
Is it clear who the author is and who has published the site?
Are they qualified to provide information on this topic?
Is the material biased?
Where is the content published? (Which country, for example.)
What is the domain name of the website?
Is it published by a large organisation, or on a personal website?
Does the website cover the topic fully?
Does it provide links and references to other materials?
If links to other materials are provided, are these evaluated or annotated to provide further information? Do these links work?
Does the site contain any advertising?
Does any advertising influence the content?

Purpose, audience and relevance

What are the aims of the site?
Does it achieve its aims?

Who is the intended audience for this content?
Is the content easy to read and understand?
Is the site specifically aimed at children? If so, is the level and tone of the content appropriate?
Is the site specifically aimed at adults?
Does the material provide everything that is needed?
Could more relevant material be found elsewhere? (In a book or magazine for example.)
Is the site trying to sell something?

Objectivity

Is the information offered as fact or opinion?
Is the information biased in any obvious way?

Accuracy and currency

Does the information appear to be accurate?
Are additional references given?
Can the information be verified from other sources?
Is the spelling and grammar correct?
Is the content dated?
When was the content last updated?
Are all links up-to-date and valid?
Are any areas of the site "under construction"?

Format

Does the site contain information in a format that I would be able to make use of?

Links

Does the site give me advice/ideas/other choices?

Ease of use

Is the site easy to use?
Is the site well structured?
Is it easy to find relevant information?
Is the content set out in an easy to use way?
What facilities does the site provide to help locate information? Does it have a search facility?
Is the menu navigation logical?
Does it provide a site map or index?
Does the site load quickly?
Is the site attractive in design?
Is the content copyright, or can it be used providing the source is acknowledged?

These questions are all pertinent and certainly deserving of attention. Obviously these questions could not easily be answered on the site of a specific activity (the activity itself should be evaluated with a set of criteria relating to educational value and suitability), but the site hosting the activity can be scrutinised and evaluated in this way. Experienced internet users often run through these points, or at least some of them, when they visit a site for the first time. The questions as they are phrased here, are not suitable for use directly by children, but it is possible to introduce the ideas and skills involved in ways which children can understand. A simple sheet to fill in can be used to encourage children to think about the issues. This need not be done as a regular feature of work with the internet, but can be very useful as a way of introducing the process. Some teachers keep a bank of website evaluations, or mini reviews, prepared by children as a resource for others.

There are many internet resources to help with the evaluation of websites. A keyword search on any search engine will provide a range of sites, and some useful tools and checklists. The ICT Advice site (http://ictadvice.org.uk) provides guidance on evaluating and reviewing websites, including some key considerations for teachers.

The National Grid for Learning provides a gateway to educational resources on the internet, through a network of selected links to websites that offer high quality content and information. It also provides links to web-based resources that can assist with evaluating websites. The national aspect of the NGfL is now closed, but its work is continued by many local versions run by Local Education Authorities.

An important pointer to the pedigree of a website, and a means of answering some of the questions above, can be found in its address (URL). For example, an address which includes the characters ".ac.uk" has its source in a British academic institution, usually a university. Table 2.2 below gives details of other elements of web addresses, which provide insight into their background and ownership.

Table 2.2   **A selection of domain codes**

Domain code	Meaning
.co	Commercial body in the UK. Used almost exclusively in the form ".co.uk"
.com	Originally intended for "commercial" bodies, but any person or organisation, commercial or otherwise, may register and use .com
.edu	Educational institutions. Mostly used in the USA and Australia.
.gov	Government departments, agencies and branches. Including local authorities.
.mil	Military bodies.
.net	Bodies and computers that represent part of the internet's infrastructure.
.nhs.uk	UK National Health Service trust or department.
.org	Designated for miscellaneous bodies that do not fit under any of the other top-level domains. Mostly used by non-profit organisations.

THE KEY FEATURES OF ICT

It is widely agreed (published in an initial format in DfES, 1998) that there are certain distinguishable features of ICT that are important in the educational use of computer technology. Some, if not all of the features also have an important bearing on the value of computer technology in all settings where it is used. They are:

- Speed
- Capacity
- Automation
- Communicability
- Replication
- Provisionality
- Interactivity
- Non-linearity
- Multi-modality

All of the above features have a bearing on the use made of ICT, in general, and the internet, in particular, by children in school. The features which have specific relevance for internet use are discussed below.

- **Speed** – ICT, and computers in particular, allows for actions and interactions to be undertaken remarkably quickly. When we consider that one aspect of computer speed is measured in "millions of instructions per second" (MIPS) we can begin to understand the notion of speed in the realm of computing. The notion of speed measured in this way can appear meaningless in the context of a child using a particular program, but what it means in practice is that it is possible to make changes and receive feedback very, very quickly. Many instructions can be acted upon quickly, for example, altering a graph, correcting a spelling, or any of the many actions involved in specific educational software. When using the internet there is a sense of immediacy and of control, the effects of which can act as a motivator for many children. Access to information from around the world can be gained in very short time frames. Messages can be sent across the world, and on occasions replies can come back in minutes or even seconds.
- **Capacity** – The internet gives access to an incredibly large amount of information across the widest possible range of topics: "… the capacity and range of ICT can enable teachers and pupils to gain access to historical, recent or immediate information." (DfES, 1998) Children are able to gain access to images, sounds and text from many different and reputable sources. It is widely accepted that the internet has taken on a form that goes far beyond the capacity of any previously accessible repository of information.
- **Communicability** – It is possible to develop means of communicating both within the classroom (by ICT mediated presentations for example) and beyond the classroom. The internet and its possibilities for e-mail, chat and messaging have opened up many possibilities for long distance rapid communication, which can be used to good educational advantage.

- **Interactivity** – The ability of ICT systems to offer and promote an interactive approach to school work is a clear advantage. When we consider the view of learning that suggests that learning is an interactive, collaborative process, depending upon communication and feedback, it is easy to recognise the advantages offered by interactive computer applications, computer mediated communication and the collaboration and discussion that can be engendered by well planned computer-related tasks. Another aspect of interactivity which ICT and the internet can provide is in the form of immediate feedback to tasks and activities that can be undertaken either from CD- or computer-based software, or via the internet.

  > ... the interactive way in which information is stored, processed and presented can enable teachers and pupils to:

  i.   explore prepared or constructed models and simulations, where relevant to the subject and phase;
  ii. communicate with other people, locally and over distances, easily and effectively;
  iii. search for and compare information from different sources;
  iv. present information in ways which are accessible in different forms for different audiences. (DfES, 1998)

- **Non-linearity** – Traditionally, information has been delivered in a linear fashion, and there are many occasions when this is highly appropriate. With the advent of hypertext style information systems it is possible for the user to navigate through what can be large volumes of information in a personal and possibly more meaningful way. Being able to gather information from a variety of ICT sources that users can navigate in their own ways, by following interests or "clues", gives a freedom to explore and find out, which has not easily been possible in the past.
- **Multi-modality** – Sound, pictures (both moving and still) can be used for teaching activities very easily. When we consider this in connection with the learning preferences of different learners, and the emphasis which is often put on what is known as multi-sensory learning (learning via a range of different human senses – sound, vision, touch and so on), we can see that there are distinct advantages for teachers when making use of this particular feature. In some cases children can respond to their experiences by using the multimodal capability of web page creation software. They could, for example, design and create a web page which incorporates pictures, video, diagrams, symbols, text and sound.

The European Schoolnet project (European Schoolnet, undated) highlights certain features, most of which are listed above, of ICT that make it particularly suitable for education, namely:

- It combines and integrates a full range of media essential for effective learning. ICT uses sound, vision, text and numeric data.
- It provides teachers and pupils with new opportunities for long distance communication and learning and an involvement in the "real world".
- There is an opportunity to increase the interest and involvement of pupils by the one-to-one relationship provided by the pupil and computer. Not all learning is necessarily done from books, and computers via ICT can act as a catalyst to interest, involvement and enthusiasm.
- It provides students with an opportunity to work and learn on their own.

Some of the features above are able to enhance learning for many. Others can be seen to work in two ways. For example, saying that ICT allows for more individual work to be undertaken seems to consider that this is a wholly desirable situation, which it might not always be. For some learners, at some times, this is perhaps ideal, but certainly not for everyone all of the time. ICT in this case offers the option for more individual and independent learning, but as we have seen, ICT related activities also allow for more collaborative and communicative work as well.

The features considered above will be evident in later chapters where specific internet use is considered in more detail.

PEDAGOGY

The word "pedagogy" has an important place in the educational lexicon, but it is not a word that is often heard spoken amongst teachers, except perhaps in the context of in-service training and even then it is not often a topic for discussion. Pedagogy is usually defined as the art, or science, of teaching, and sometimes the profession of teaching. For both Gage (1985) and Simon (1994) it is somehow both: "The science of the art of teaching." At the same time, both Woods (1996) and Reynolds (1998) see it as science. Pedagogy refers to the teaching of children and its sister word "andragogy" refers to the teaching of adults.

Teachers apply pedagogic principles in a wide range of settings with an equally wide range of groups and individuals who present many varied challenges. Executing a pedagogical approach depends to a large extent on the judgement of the professional teacher and the practical skills that the teacher has learned and practised. This is put succinctly by Galton: "… an effective pedagogy requires that educational theory needs to be integrated with teacher's craft knowledge, that is knowledge of what works in practice" (Galton, 2000: 1).

Mortimore (1999: 17) describes pedagogical activity as, "Any conscious activity by one person designed to enhance learning in another", which clearly includes decisions made by teachers, and to an extent by policy makers, concerning the place of new technologies in teaching and learning.

So "pedagogy" has come to refer to the skills and approaches used by teachers to achieve the aims of the lessons that they teach, or the methods which they employ. These methods vary from teacher to teacher and from time to time according to the nature of the subject being taught, or the possible responses of the children being taught. When new facilities or equipment are to be used this can lead to a new or different pedagogical approach being adopted. This has, to some extent, been the case with the advent of ICT in schools and with the use of the internet.

Teachers have theories and systems of beliefs concerning teaching, and the way in which learning takes place that influence their approach to teaching. Decisions which teachers take before, during and after teaching a lesson have a deep influence on the learning that takes place in their classrooms. (Fennema and Franke, 1992). Although precisely "what to teach" is often prescribed for teachers, through the medium of a national curriculum or some other mandatory document, precisely how to teach it, how to organise the children and the classroom for teaching is something which is generally left to the teacher to decide. (The literacy and numeracy strategies for UK primary schools are notable exceptions.) Such decisions as when to work with the whole class or when to work with a group or an individual, who to choose to answer a question, whether pupils should work alone, in pairs or in small groups, what style of resource to use and what nature of support should be offered and when, are just a sample of the decisions that teachers are engaged with on a regular basis. This is when teachers are involved in the consideration of pedagogy.

Alexander (1992) identifies teaching methods and pupil organisation as the two facets of pedagogy. Both of these facets demand consideration when a teacher is faced with making use of a new technology if its full value is to be found.

Teachers tend not to refer to pedagogy explicitly because they are intimately involved with the practical application of pedagogy through their planning and teaching on a daily basis, and what they plan and implement is closely related to their internalisation of how to teach and how children best learn. Teachers are at the place where theory becomes practice and they do not spend time considering the niceties, or otherwise, of theoretical "advice". They concentrate more on the craft skills which Galton (2000) refers to, and to providing activities and contexts that will encourage learning. Teachers do talk about and consider how they introduced a topic, how they approached teaching a particular subject, how they grouped children, how they explained something, how they expected the children to respond to the work, and much more. Their thought, discussion and new ideas are based upon what has gone before, including theoretical perspectives, and what has been learned from empirical classroom based research, but it is the practical, day to day planning and organisation that engages teachers more than a philosophical discussion. Later in this book we will see how teachers have applied their knowledge and understanding of pedagogy, along with well developed craft skills, to provide rich and successful learning environments. All of this, of course, does amount to a consideration of pedagogy.

TRADITIONAL PEDAGOGIES: HOW TEACHERS THINK ABOUT THEIR APPROACHES TO TEACHING

In the traditions of the past, the Victorian age for example, the prevailing view on teaching and learning was that children's heads were empty and it was the job of the teacher to remedy that by filling them with information in the form of facts. Mr Gradgrind in Dickens' *Hard Times* (1891) makes this viewpoint brutally obvious: "Teach these boys and girls nothing but facts. Facts alone are wanted in life." This philosophy is expounded at length by the fearsome school master, but even he eventually comes to a realisation of the possible folly of this approach.

In terms of pedagogy we have come a long way since the times of Thomas Gradgrind, but there is still no single pedagogy that is accepted and pursued by all. There is a recognition that for different children, different subject matter and different times of day even, different approaches to teaching are required. This is partly owing to a recognition that there is indeed more to a broad and balanced education than the acquisition of facts, and also a result of the wealth of knowledge that has been accrued over the last century concerning the ways in which effective learning is facilitated, and indeed by the development of appropriate definitions of learning.

CHILD-CENTRED VERSUS TEACHER-CENTRED PEDAGOGIES

There has been a history of polarisation and of a swinging pendulum between a so-called "back to basics" approach, where government ministers proclaimed the benefits of teachers "standing at the front and teaching", and a more liberal approach with the curriculum "beginning with the child". These movements in education necessarily have an effect on the way teachers think about their teaching and the way that they approach their work in classrooms. As long ago as the sixteenth century the writer Rabelais believed a child to be: "... a fire to be lit, not a vessel to be filled". When this is contrasted with the Victorian view we see a perfect example of the pendulum swing.

At a simplistic level the two extreme positions that lead to an individual teacher defining a personal pedagogical approach to teaching could be described in terms of the belief that either children are empty vessels which need to be filled, or that children are thinking individuals who are ready and eager to build an understanding of the world around them. In reality of course it is not so simple. Many teachers' beliefs lie at a point on the continuum between the two extremes. According to contextual factors such as the topic being taught, the nature or age of the children, the teacher's understanding of the subject matter, the availability of resources, even, as we have said, the time of day, the pedagogy employed by an individual may shift one way or the other from time to time. Sometimes this change in approach is referred to as "fitness for purpose" and supposes that different teaching purposes are better achieved by one particular teaching approach or another.

We will look briefly at four pedagogies put forward by Bruner (1996) before moving to consider the demands made on teachers' pedagogical practice by the advent of new technologies, including the internet.

Bruner's folk pedagogies

Bruner points out that there are four views concerning teaching that seem to be held by teachers and others involved in education. He refers to them as "folk pedagogies", implying that they are not necessarily based upon research or theory, but developed as a result of personal experience of schooling and of teaching.

Of the four pedagogies that Bruner suggests that most teachers subscribe to, there are two which can be seen to be in line with constructivist thinking on learning and two which cannot. The first two involve children being expected to copy or imitate those who have successfully acquired a particular skill, or competence, and secondly, children being told specific facts and being expected to internalise them – a far more passive process than constructivists would advocate, and more definitely within the behaviourist domain. Bruner's third and fourth pedagogies take the nature of the child and the child's state of knowledge and awareness into account and also imply some sort of activity on the part of the learner.

The four folk pedagogies are:

1. *Seeing children as imitative learners: the acquisition of "know how"*
    The learner learns by being shown and then copying others. Referred to as the "apprenticeship model", learning is considered to be the transmission of skills and competences. This model does not stress the passing on of knowledge. Bruner tells us that research suggests that imitation is not enough. Procedural

knowledge, which is the knowledge of how to perform a particular task, is best suited to this style of learning.

2. *Seeing children as learning from didactic exposure: the acquisition of proposi-
    tional knowledge*
    This pedagogy suggests that learning is a matter of being told; information is
    passed on from the one who knows to those who do not. "Knowledge is ...
    'looked up' or 'listened to' ..." (Bruner, 1996: 55). Bruner says that this is the
    most commonly held view of learning. It ignores learning that has gone before and
    sees the process as essentially passive. Propositional knowledge is knowledge that
    a given idea, or proposition, is either true or false.

3. *Seeing children as thinkers: the development of intersubjective interchange*
    According to this notion of learning the learner is actively engaged in the con-
    struction of meaning. "The teacher, on this view, is concerned with understanding
    what the child thinks ... understanding is fostered through discussion and collabo-
    ration ..." (Bruner, 1996: 56). Learning is seen as a collaborative enterprise both
    between learners, and between teachers and learners. This view is criticised because
    of its depiction of knowledge, suggesting that knowledge is something learners con-
    struct for themselves. Intersubjectivity refers to shared understanding, which can be
    constructed by individuals in their exchanges with others.

4. *Children as knowledgeable: the management of "objective" knowledge*
    Bruner suggests that "teaching should help children grasp the distinction
    between personal knowledge, on the one side and 'what is taken to be known'
    by the culture on the other" (1996: 61). Objective knowledge is knowledge that
    is universally agreed upon, or at least virtually agreed – we cannot easily take
    into account the views of those who believe the Earth to be flat for example.
    Learners become aware of the cultural setting of knowledge, and also become
    aware of what is "known" by others. This is done in a variety of ways, for
    example, through texts and other artefacts. The process involves dialogue.

It is possible to see a range of different uses of ICT being involved with and being
supported by pedagogies from all four of these models at different times and in vary-
ing circumstances.

For example, Rodrigues (1997) looked at the use of Integrated Learning Systems (ILSs)
by able pupils. An ILS is a computer based system of programmed learning which leads
the learner through a series of activities, tasks and tests, monitors progress and devises
individualised learning routes. Rodrigues recognised that the use of an ILS is based on
the "mastery" approach to learning and modelled on an "expert's notion of hierarchical
difficulty" (1997: 125). The approach taken when teaching with the help of an ILS is
based on Bruner's first and second models: learners as imitative, and learning from didactic exposure. The use of an ILS does not require discussion or consultation with others.

Computer use is often undertaken by children working in groups and there has been
a good deal of research into group work with ICT. This research is, in most cases, set
in the context of constructivist learning theory, and in line with Bruner's third model
in which children are considered as thinkers in their own right. The teacher has an
important role in this style of learning as the planner, instigator and more importantly
as the manager of the learning context. The teacher also takes on the role of partner

in dialogue in many cases, intervening at appropriate times and providing scaffolding of differing types and levels of complexity.

The Teacher Training Agency (TTA, 1999) studied the approaches taken by a sample of teachers. They identified the set of characteristics below which teachers using ICT effectively, in terms of children's learning, had in common.

- A positive rather than a negative attitude towards ICT.
- A preference for pupil choice rather than teacher direction.
- A preference for pupil control over their own learning rather than teacher delivering the curriculum by instruction.
- A preference for individual study as opposed to whole group instruction.

We have now seen that teachers' approaches to their teaching can be wide and varied and that specific approaches may depend upon a number of factors, some of which are determined by training and experience, others by the context of the teaching. The introduction of new technologies in recent years, and the increasing obligation to integrate its use in the classroom, can be seen as yet another contextual factor. For some teachers this has presented problems, either of confidence or concerning the understanding of the place of technology in teaching and learning. It has led to some teachers questioning and redefining elements of their work – their pedagogy. For some teachers the principles which they have applied in their work have not altered, and they have integrated technology use at the same time as adhering to constructivist principles. This has lead to the introduction and development of new and valuable learning experiences for pupils, adhering in some cases to less child-centred beliefs. Other teachers have varied their approaches and allowed the use of certain computer programs to refer back to more behaviourist approaches to learning – drill and practice; ILS. One commentator considered that the introduction of computers into classrooms had allowed for a backward step to be taken when he said: "The microcomputer is a tool of awesome potency which is making it possible for educational practice to take a giant step backwards." (Chandler, 1984: 1) Chandler is suggesting that some of the outdated drill and practice style learning situations, for example learning by rote, which often ignores notions of understanding, might experience a rebirth through the work of the educational software creators who, at the time when he was writing at least, seemed to know little about more enlightened approaches to learning. Software design, including the design of activities mediated through the internet, have come a long way since then.

One important development in the pedagogy involved in greater use of the internet is the increased opportunity for and use of interactive modes of working. There are certain "… pedagogical changes that electronic technologies make possible. The word that captures them best is interactivity."(Furr, 2003: 2)

The Department for Education and Skills (DfES) provide a list of constructivist characteristics. The suggestion is that if lessons involving the use of the internet are to be effective, and at the same time address elements of the national curriculum for ICT concerning the development of the qualities of independent learning, they should exhibit some of these characteristics. Obviously it would not be realistic to expect lessons to include all of these characteristics, but some lessons might well have many of them present in some measure at least.

Characteristics of constructivist learning that might be present in ICT related lessons include:

- multiple perspectives
- pupil-directed goals
- teachers as coaches
- metacognition
- learner control
- real-world activities and contexts
- knowledge construction
- sharing knowledge
- reference to what pupils know already
- problem solving
- explicit thinking about errors and misconceptions
- exploration
- peer-group learning
- alternative viewpoints offered
- scaffolding
- assessment for learning
- primary sources of data.

(DfES, 2004b)

This list, from the arm of the UK government responsible for the curriculum in schools and for ensuring high standards amongst pupils, is clearly promoting a constructivist approach to learning with ICT. This coincides with Bruner's pedagogies three and four: children as active constructors and children as knowledgeable. It also gives a clear steer away from more behaviouristic approaches to ICT use such as the repetitive drill and practice, or revision style activities that were so prevalent in the 1980s and early 1990s. It will be interesting and useful to measure the case studies in later chapters against this list and to consider the characteristics of the teaching that is deemed to have been effective. In this way we will be able to recognise and promote good pedagogical practice in the area of ICT use generally, and the internet in particular.

NCREL (undated) draws attention to research that is taking place into how to capitalise on the increased use of computers in education and the increase in easy internet access. The research is focusing on aspects of what seems to be happening already, and into ways of extending what is considered to be good practice, namely more

- engaged, meaningful learning and collaboration involving challenging and real-life tasks and
- opportunities to use technology as a tool for learning, communication and collaboration.

This too is in line with the apparent shift towards the use of ICT in constructivist learning settings, and towards a pedagogy that emphasises the use of technology to support learners in making use of the existing technologies as important tools for effective learning.

Taking all of this into account, it is important to keep in mind the notion that any new development in pedagogy deemed necessary to make effective use of new technologies in teaching and learning situations must continue to emphasise learning, and not fall into the trap of emphasising and focusing on the technology. This was recognised many years ago by Ellis (1974) when he said that: "Thinking about the computer's role in education does not mean thinking about computers, it means thinking about education." (1974: 42) This is as true now as it was when it was written. ICT is a powerful tool when it is used as an aid to learning and when it has a supporting, not a central, role in the process of classroom learning.

SUMMARY

The internet is, for all intents and purposes, available to all teachers in all schools. As such it is available as a resource for teaching and learning, and as with all tools and resources used in classrooms, its use should be carefully considered. Not only should the approaches to teaching and learning be looked at in detail, as we did in chapter one, but the integrity and usefulness of individual websites should also be carefully investigated.

There are certain features of ICT which can have a big impact on teaching and learning. Features such as speed, capacity, automation, communicability, replication, provisionality, interactivity, non-linearity and multi-modality can be used to good advantage, but a shift in the pedagogical approaches taken by teachers to do this, and can make a very big difference to the ways in which both teachers and children are able to work.

An individual teacher may subscribe to a particular preferred approach to their teaching that will have been developed in the light of their own learning, and the experiences had in their job. Certain approaches may suit different teaching contexts, and different individual learners more than others. Teachers need to be aware that their preferred approach might not always be the most appropriate when they come to make more extensive use of the internet and other new technologies.

There are some well rehearsed characteristics of constructivist learning that might be present in effective internet related and other ICT dependant lessons. These include the use of primary sources of data, dealing with multiple perspectives, having pupil-directed goals, a degree of learner control, the use of real-world activities and contexts, the construction of knowledge rather than the presentation of facts, detailed reference to what pupils already know, problem solving, thinking about errors and misconceptions, scaffolding techniques provided by the teacher and sometimes by others, and well established formative assessment for learning.

3 Working Individually

About this chapter

Even with many changes in classroom practice over the last twenty years and more, individual work is still a mainstay of teaching methodology for many teachers. The internet offers many opportunities for individual exploration and activity, and some of these opportunities will be explored in the case studies in this chapter.

The themes that you will encounter in this chapter are:

- children working alone
- constructivism and behaviourism working together to good effect.

Questions to keep in mind when reading this chapter

- Does lone working detract from or add to the learning experiences of the children?
- Would more collaborative work improve the experiences of the children and lead to increased effective learning?
- When is working alone likely to be of most benefit to learners?
- Were the planned learning outcomes achieved in an effective way, and could they have been achieved better by some other means?

Despite much research carried out over many years, and despite the current received wisdom about collaborative work involving discussion, cooperation and shared goals, many classrooms are characterised by children working individually and with the expectation that there is little or even no need for talking. Clearly there are times when individual work is necessary and when children should know to work alone and to be quiet. Calm and quiet classrooms can lead to the production of very good work and can lead to effective learning. There is also, as we have seen, a need for sharing and working together. There are times when computer use should be a shared activity and there are also times for carrying out learning activities alone with a computer.

We will see examples in this chapter of children working alone to good effect. Two of the case studies are in the area of mathematics, and one in the area of geography. It is likely that all three of these activities could have been undertaken in a shared collaborative way, but in each case the teacher involved had made the decision to ask the children to work alone. In the case study involving Builder Ted, the teacher, quite aware of the value of discussion in her normal way of working, was clear that she wanted no talking and no collaborative working. She wanted a contrast to the way that she usually encouraged her class to work and she saw the value of a more solitary approach to the work for the particular aims that she had in mind. We will see that there is a socially constructive element to the activities in these case studies, even if the teacher tells us that there is not.

In all cases there are times when the teacher allows for feedback and reflection on what has been done – sometimes this is a part of the learning plan, and sometimes it is not. In most classrooms today it is natural and allowable for children to speak and to offer their ideas and interpretations, even when not asked for them. For this reason teachers who would prefer certain times without talk and sharing out loud find themselves allowing it to happen and in many cases recognising its value: "Yes I do want them to get on with it on their own … but when they talk and I listen in I can see that they're talking about the work and sometimes helping each other." In situations where talk has not been encouraged, or even asked for, it is likely that when it does take place it can serve to strengthen the value of the work which was to have been undertaken alone.

Case study 3.1   Drilling for tables

School

Single form entry primary school.

Teacher

Female, began teaching 24 years ago, took career break in order to be with family.

Class

Year 4 (29 pupils)

Website

Quia: www.quia.com

Background/Context

The teacher considered that the class had particularly poor knowledge of and ability to make use of multiplication facts. She pointed to the results of a series of tests from the autumn term as evidence.

The school had paid for a subscription to Quia, an American based, on-line, resources centre providing activities and downloadable materials across a very wide range of school subjects. Originally the school signed up to Quia for access to MFL resources as part of a pilot scheme for teaching Spanish in a primary school. The year 6 class were taught Spanish by a visiting teacher and Quia was used as reinforcement and extension work. The teacher in year 4 became aware of the maths resources provided by Quia by chance in a conversation with her colleague. As a result of this the school staff were introduced to Quia and most of the classes made at least some use of the resources. The year 4 teacher made extensive use of the "drill and practice" style activities in the maths area.

Quia

The Quia website makes the bold statement that it is: "The Web's leading technology resource for educators." (2006) Quia, which we are told is pronounced "key-ah", is an abbreviation for

(Continued)

(Continued)

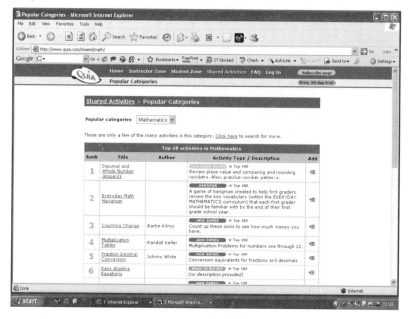

Figure 3.1   **Part of the activities list in Quia for mathematics**

"Quintessential Instructional Archive". It is a subscription service for schools that provides a very wide range of online activities and resources for the years of compulsory education.

One of the features of the site is that it allows for the creation of activities based on templates that are provided. This feature also allows any activities created by members to be made available to others on the site. In practice this means that the resource bank is very large and growing at a steady rate. It also means that the resources are, for the most part, created by teachers to meet a specific need and for that reason likely to be of particular interest to other teachers. This is not to undermine the activities provided by the site owners, which are generally of a high quality.

There is a collection of shared online activities and quizzes in more than 150 categories, and for each topic there are downloadable resources that can be used in conjunction with the online activities as reinforcement and in most cases as extension work.

The site is organised around 16 different types of activities, and in general the focus is on an approach related to rote learning. There is little activity that could be considered as direct teaching but, when used in conjunction with other activities and approaches, a blend of different types of teaching and learning can be achieved. The behaviourist principles encapsulated in the basic approach taken by the activities on the site are supported by opportunities to look at correct responses and to revise and recap. Ample opportunity for practice is given and, indeed, recommended. The resources for each activity include flashcards, matching and concentration games (many will recognise the matching and concentration games as versions of the traditional game of pelmanism, sometimes known as "pairs") and word searches.

A subscription gives access to: templates for creating 16 different types of online activities, including flashcards, matching, concentration (memory), word search, battleship, challenge board, columns, close exercises, hangman, jumbled words, ordered list, patterns, picture perfect, pop-ups, rags to riches (a quiz show style trivia game, recognisable as the television game "Who wants to be a millionaire?"), and scavenger hunt.

There is also access to tools for creating online quizzes with ten different types of question, including multiple choice, true/false, pop-up, multiple correct (where there can be a selection of correct responses), fill-in (requiring free text answers), matching and ordering.

(Continued)

There are a number of management and reporting tools available which allow the subscriber to keep a close record on the activities and progress of individual users.

To use some of the basic activities provided by the site there is no need to subscribe. However to make use of the more advanced features which are provided, such as the extensive record keeping possibilities and the features that allow the creation and sharing of new resources, a subscription is needed.

Teacher's prior knowledge and experience

The teacher had limited experience of computer use with children except for encouraging, fairly extensively, the use of a word processor for writing tasks and the use of a spelling program (Star Spell) for the least able children in the class to practise their weekly spellings. She had been helped in the past to set up a database for a project on minibeasts, but did not feel confident enough to do it alone. She used the internet for both professional and personal reasons and was in touch with relatives overseas by e-mail.

Children's prior knowledge/experience

All of the children had access to a computer at home and most reported using it for games and a few for "chat". Some had found information for school-related work, and some had word-processed short homework assignments. In school the children had been exposed to word processing in every year so far, as well as the use of a Logo style program in year 1, painting and drawing and a simple spreadsheet activity in year 2, graphing results in a science experiment in year 3, and the use of a simple adventure/problem solving game at the beginning of year 4.

In terms of their experience with learning tables, this had been to greater and lesser degree, a feature of their work in every class. During the current school year they had been given learning tasks to complete at home and weekly tests. Despite this the teacher still felt that the children were not making the sort of progress that she expected.

Format of the use of Quia

The teacher saw the use of the Quia activities as an essential element of the learning of multiplication facts. By "learning" she actually meant "memorising". In itself this was not a bad aim for this type of activity, but if an understanding of the nature of multiplication and the relationships between numbers and arithmetic operations was to be achieved, many would agree that there was need for more than the activities provided by the website. The teacher seemed to recognise this and said that she had viewed it as a small, but important, part of the children's full mathematical experience.

Each week every child spent some time using the site. There was a rota pinned to the wall near to the computer and the class knew to notify the next person on the list when they had finished. The children themselves kept a record of what they had done, and they were expected to print out any pages where they had succeeded in getting everything right.

Response of the children

The children were generally enthusiastic about the use of Quia and showed this when told that it was their turn to use the site. When using the activities there was clear concentration, and for many what seemed like obvious determination to succeed.

(Continued)

(Continued)

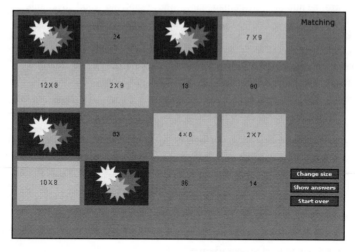

Figure 3.2   **An example screen from a matching activity in Quia**

At spare moments some of the class chose to look through the other options that were available, including:

1. Computer Basics – How well do you know the parts of the computer? Play this game to check your level of knowledge of the computer and its related equipment.
2. Hangman.

Many of the games and quizzes looked at during free time were too difficult for most children, but they persisted and liked to make wild guesses rather than give up and leave the computer to someone else.

Views and response of the teacher involved

The teacher had taken to using these activities with some enthusiasm despite her initial reluctance.

> Everyone has a session at least once a week. It is simply a question of practise and more practise – there is no real teaching going on. They all work at a level where they have been having trouble ... there was a test before we started and it showed them which one (multiplication table) to start with.
>   We have developed a "Leader Board" something that I have avoided in the past because of the effect on self esteem for those at the bottom ... The way that it works is to give stars next to names, each child is working at their own level and everyone has the potential to be successful and get up with the leaders ... It has generated so much interest that I can't keep them away from it.
>   I think, but it's not that easy to know ... that it has led to an improvement in the use of numbers in other numeracy lessons ... when we started area last term someone immediately pointed out that the numbers were being multiplied were 'Just like in Quia' ... it's making connections like this ... that makes a difference.

The teacher asked the children to print out each page that was all correct and put them in a folder of evidence. Some children had several printed pages of the same page completed

(Continued)

on different occasions, which she considered a good approach as it meant that they had revisited the same activity more than once and practised well. She recognised the fact that the inclusion of correct pages in a folder was not a measure of success. Trial and error can soon lead to a page of correct responses, but she liked the idea that the children had a record, and she could see what they had been working on when she collected in the maths folders. She did not make use of the record keeping options within Quia.

Another feature of the software that suited the teacher was that there was no excessive fanfare of celebration when an exercise was completed successfully:

> I can't stand the commotion that some programs make when a right answer is given, which is why I won't use some of them ... (that we have in school).

One point that detracted slightly from the teacher's enthusiasm for the site was the fact that the site is from the USA, and therefore littered with cultural references from North America, such as the coins referred to, the use of American presidents as examples, and the use of both American spellings and of American terminology, for example sidewalk. This was not a problem with multiplication and other simple basics, and the teacher simply did not use any activities which were not suitable for any of the reasons above.

Evidence of learning

The teacher was clear that motivation and interest in the use of the computer for these activities soared, and this had led to an all round improvement in attainment across the whole class. She is able to claim this with some certainty because she had the results of tests that she had carried out on a weekly basis and also a more expansive test at the ends of the term. She also points to an apparent improvement in the mental oral starter session of numeracy lessons for evidence. She often used "quick fire" multiplication questions as an introduction and she was sure that both response times and correct answers had improved through the term.

Pedagogical and theoretical considerations

The mathematical activities on the Quia website that the children worked on were essentially designed for practise and reinforcement, and as such can be placed towards the behaviourist end of what can be seen as a continuum between constructivist and behaviourist learning. There are, however, more extreme versions of behaviourist learning than these. As we have seen, behaviourist style learning looks for the ability to recall, in this context, and does not stress understanding. One of the teacher's aims was to increase this ability, but she also wanted to improve the abilities of the class in using multiplication facts "intelligently and appropriately". To this end she encouraged a little discussion in whole-class sessions and drew attention to methods for working out particular answers if they were not instantly "recallable".

The teacher said that there was little actual teaching taking place when the activities were underway, and this too is a feature of behaviourist learning. The element of competition and the use of a "leader board" is also behaviouristic in nature.

Connections that can be made between different areas of learning, and especially with previous learning, have an important part to play in constructing knowledge and understanding and the teacher was able to encourage this. It is interesting also to see that children were making connections of their own: "It's like in Quia."

(Continued)

(Continued)

Table 3.1   **Characteristics of constructivist learning that might be present in ICT related lessons: Drilling for tables**

Multiple perspectives		
Pupil-directed goals		
Teachers as coaches		
Metacognition	✓	Partly – children encouraged to think about how to "remember" the right answers. Some seen to be working out answers and not relying on recall. When asked about it they explained how they were counting on and so on. Some discussion of "method" occasionally in plenary sessions.
Learner control	✓	Yes, children can choose where to go next – encouraged to complete each "level" more than once (five is best) but they choose when to move on.
Real-world activities and contexts		
Knowledge construction	✓	
Sharing knowledge	✓	Some discussion of "method" occasionally in plenary sessions (See "Metacognition".)
Reference to what pupils know already	✓	
Problem solving	✓	
Explicit thinking about errors and misconceptions	✓	
Exploration		
Peer-group learning	✓	Some discussion; minimal.
Alternative viewpoints offered		
Scaffolding	✓	Not really, but work is pitched at correct level of difficulty.
Assessment for learning		
Primary sources of data		

Table 3.2   **Drilling for tables: Other considerations/features**

Motivation	✓	Yes, all very obvious.
Enjoyment	✓	
Excitement	✓	
Novelty	✓	
Engagement	✓	
Development of work away from the computer	✓	Minimal – the facts covered and practised are referred to in other number contexts.
Evidence of learning	✓	Yes – end of term test; evidence in other areas of maths work.

Does the use of the infrastructure of the internet in this example extend the possibilities for learning beyond what would have been expected if the content of the lesson had been covered in a more traditional way?

The activities that the children use in this example are based on simple games that have existed for a very long time, easily pre-dating the use of computers in school. It is true that the teacher could have arranged for the games to be played with cards and pre-prepared score sheets, but what is also clear is that the children were very highly motivated by these "computerised" versions of the simple games. The teacher says that "Before using the Quia games I found it very difficult to generate any interest at all in improving multiplication

(Continued)

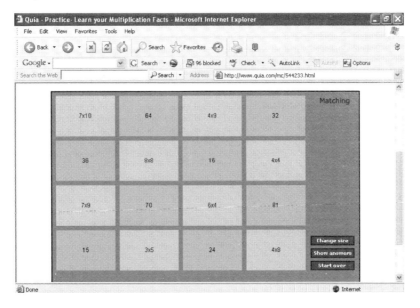

Figure 3.3   **An example of a Quia screen**

facts – this has made a big difference." On its own, as we have seen previously, motivation cannot be a sole justification for the use of computer technology for something that can be done more easily without. In this case the teacher is convinced that the improvement in both attitude and attainment in the area under consideration is a result of the extended use of the online programs. For her this is all of the justification that she needs to continue in the same vein. Indeed, if the children are better motivated, and if they engage with the work well at the same time as measurable learning improvements, there is a real justification for its use.

Case study 3.2   Builder Ted and decimals

School

Large three form entry equivalent urban primary school.

Teacher

Female with considerable experience. She is the deputy head of the school and has been a maths coordinator in the past. She has used computers in her teaching for many years, but very little in the context of numeracy.

Class

Year 6 (29 pupils), top "set" of three for numeracy.

(Continued)

(Continued)

Figure 3.4   **The opening screen of a Builder Ted activity, showing the ladder where the bricks have to be placed in the correct order**

Website

BBC: www.bbc.co.uk/education/mathsfile/shockwave/games/laddergame.html

Background/Context and children's prior knowledge/experience

The year group is "set" for numeracy lessons and the group in question is a high ability group. All of the children have good mathematical knowledge and ability. During numeracy lessons earlier in the term the teacher found that the group's understanding of place value was generally good, but they found difficulty with ordering positive and negative numbers with two or more decimal places. The teacher used the game "Builder Ted" as a way of practising and reinforcing certain key ideas.

There were two computers available for this work in the classroom, and another two in a shared work area adjacent to the classroom.

Web-based activity

The activity Builder Ted gives practice in ordering decimal numbers in the form of an animated game. It is part of a set of games-like activities included on the BBC's Maths File Game Show site. (BBC, 2002)

The activity allows children to make choices about the order of numbers in the context of helping a builder to climb a ladder. The activity can be at one of three levels of difficulty and includes both background information, and tips for completing the task.

(Continued)

Tips

First decide which numbers are positive and which are negative. Then look at the digit furthest to the left.
The largest positive number is the one with the largest number furthest to the left.
The rule reverses for negative numbers.
All positive numbers are larger than all negative numbers.

Place value

Place value is the basis of our number system. The position of a digit gives it its value.
The digits further to the left have larger values than those to the right.
For example, 234
The 2 is in the "hundreds" column, and has the value of 200.
The 3 is in the "tens" column, and has the value of 30.
The 4 is in the "units" column, and has the value of 4.

Decimals

Decimals are a continuation of the number system, and the decimal point marks the change from whole numbers to fractions.
For example, 6.49
6 is in the "units" column, and has a value of 6.
4 is in the "tenths" column, and has a value of 4/10.
9 is in the "hundredths" column, and has a value of 9/100.

Figure 3.5 **Some of the "Tips" from the activity**

The background information was considered important to the teacher because she did not want to simply present an activity to the group, she wanted something that had the potential to support and teach. That is, she did not want to put the children in a position where they might fail and not be able to learn from the experience. She also wanted to encourage a measure of independence, which she felt this activity would allow.

The site is actually aimed at an older age group, key stage 3, but the teacher was confident that it was appropriate for this higher ability group.

If a mistake is made the pupil has to go back to the beginning. The third time a mistake is made the answers are given and the pupil is prompted to start again.

After a successful attempt a prize is offered, as a print out, with the promise of a better prize if the next level is completed – vinyl washable stool, Elizabethan false teeth, pair of wooden antlers.

The site offers downloadable support materials to be printed and used as extension work.

Builder Ted was used as a contrasting activity and as a reminder about work on decimals and positive/negative numbers. Everyone had a turn during the week's numeracy lessons. The theme of the lessons was not related to the topic of the game, but work on ordering integers had been covered earlier in the term as part of some of the mental oral starters.

To introduce the work the teacher used the classroom's projector and screen to go through ways of using the software. She also spent a good deal of time looking at and discussing the two areas of the site designed to give support. She wanted to use this as a reminder of the principles involved, and also wanted to be sure that the children would know where to find

(Continued)

(Continued)

Placing numbers in order of size

When comparing the size of two numbers, we always look at the digits furthest to the left. For example, which is bigger, 135 or 137?

The numbers in the "hundreds" and "tens" columns are the same, but when we compare the "units" column, we see that 7 is bigger than 5. Therefore, 137 is bigger than 135. For example, which is bigger, 4.2 or 4.07?

The numbers in the "units" columns are the same, but when we compare the "tenths" column, we see that 2 is bigger than 0. Therefore, 4.2 is bigger than 4.07.

Negative numbers

Positive numbers are greater than 0.
Negative numbers are less than 0.
−6 −5 −4 −3 −2 −1 0 1 2 3 4 5 6
We always count away from 0, so 6 is greater than 4, but −6 is less than −4.
For example, place the numbers 5, −7, −2, −5, 1 in order of size, smallest first.
−7, −5, −2, 1, 5

Figure 3.6   **Part of the background information from the activity, which was used with the whole class as an introduction**

help if they felt that it was needed. She asked them to read through the "Key Ideas" text and the "Helpful Tips" before they started to use the game when it was their turn.

Children worked alone trying to complete all three levels and printed out the top prize as evidence of their success. Some trial and error went on at first, but this approach didn't allow the prizes to be won and always stopped further progress by giving the correct answer. As each child became familiar with what was required, they became more intent on getting it right.

Support and scaffolding was available from two sources. Firstly the "Tips" and "Key Ideas" links from the activity itself, and secondly by referring to the teacher. It was made clear that if there was a problem the first port of call would be the help provided by the activity and not the teacher, although she would give help if called upon. When it came to the times when children were working with the game the teacher was not asked for any help at all.

Response of the children

When the help and support pages were introduced to the class, without having first been given a chance to look at the game, there was a slight hint of disinterest amongst the group. This was not a difficult situation to deal with – the class were generally attentive and responded to questions when asked. The atmosphere in the room changed when the screen with the activity was first shown. Both body language and the buzz of excited talk was evidence of this. The animation in the activity, although repetitive, is amusing, and this clearly helped in attracting and then keeping the attention of the group.

Even though the children worked alone there were times when they spoke aloud and showed signs of delight, excitement and disappointment when working through the tasks. There were two computers next to each other in both of the locations where the computers were sited and so at most times there were two children sitting close to one another but working

(Continued)

independently. Despite the independent nature of the work there was interaction between the two children as they worked. Sometimes this was to do with the nature of the problem, sometimes to laugh together at part of the animation, and sometimes to draw attention to the prize that had been won. In one or two isolated cases the interaction involved one child asking for help. This was freely given as long as the child being asked was not too involved in their own work.

All of the children reported enjoying the work, and were able to describe in a detailed way what they had been doing. They were also able to give simple, accurate guidance to an imaginary child having difficulty with the work. One child was fairly certain that he had improved: "You don't realise it, but you getter better at it. I can do all of them dead fast now and no mistakes." Some of the children had explored the site further and had found that there were other activities in other topic areas. As a result of this the teacher was continually asked if they could use the other activities.

Views and response of the teacher involved

At the end of the week in which all of the children in the group had used the game the teacher was asked to review and evaluate its use. She realised then that she had been involved very little with its use. She had been aware of the work going on, she had been aware of the organisational aspects of the work, and she had seen many of the printed out "prizes". But she had not been called upon to give help with the content of the activity. She realised that she was not in a position to say whether the activity had served the purpose that she had intended. She assumed that it had received the approval of the group and considered this to be a good indicator of its worth. However, she was concerned that she had no measure of its success in terms of meeting the outcomes that she had in mind, namely an improvement in the ability to work with the numbers involved and a more secure understanding of decimal numbers.

During the mental/oral starters of the numeracy lessons in the following week the teacher spent time reviewing and, in a subtle way, testing the abilities of the group in terms of understanding better and being more competent when dealing with the relative sizes of positive and negative decimal numbers. Having done this she felt that the value of the activity was clear. She considered that there had been a marked improvement amongst the group in their ability to manipulate and order positive and negative decimal numbers.

The teacher was not concerned by the fact that there was little or no discussion involved in the work. Her view was that there are many opportunities in her numeracy lessons for discussion and there are times when independent work is desirable. She did concede that the activity might have been improved by building in a measure of collaboration – working in pairs and stressing the need to agree on how to proceed, but was content with the way that it had worked and would probably not change this if she used it again in the future.

Pedagogical and theoretical considerations

The teacher was clear that this was work to be done alone and she did not encourage any discussion or collaboration. However it was not a hard and fast rule. With children sitting next to each other, though working separately, there were many times when words were exchanged. These short exchanges were for different reasons. Sometimes simply to share the enjoyment of the game and at other times to consider the nature of the work. Even with the instructions to work alone there was spontaneous interaction, some of which included mutual support.

(Continued)

(Continued)

Table 3.3 **Characteristics of constructivist learning that might be present in ICT related lessons: Builder Ted and decimals**

Multiple perspectives		
Pupil-directed goals		
Teachers as coaches	✓	Initially in the introduction to the game, relating to both the use of the game and the mechanics of the mathematical method.
Metacognition	✓	Methods referred to at the end of the work and so not helpful when the work was actually being done. Teacher pointed out the "Tips" and the "Key Ideas" but most children did not need to, or at least, chose not to, use them.
Learner control	✓	Partly, moving to the next level.
Real-world activities and contexts	✓	Context of repairing a roof.
Knowledge construction	✓	Not to a great extent.
Sharing knowledge	✓	Only formally at the end of the work when everyone had finished, but incidentally with the children sitting close to each other.
Reference to what pupils know already	✓	In the context of what had been looked at previously. In hindsight the teacher thought that she could have made more of this.
Problem solving	✓	At a simple level only.
Explicit thinking about errors and misconceptions	✓	Children were asked to consider the misconceptions and reasons for mistakes in the following week's mental/oral sessions.
Exploration		
Peer-group learning	✓	To a small degree in the plenary sessions of the following week.
Alternative viewpoints offered	✓	In terms of individuals describing their methods.
Scaffolding	✓	"Tips" available if needed; not used by many. Teacher support and intervention planned for but in the event not needed.
Assessment for learning	✓	Informally mainly in the mental/oral sessions the following week. One or two written examples were used as well.
Primary sources of data		

Table 3.4   **Builder Ted and decimals: Other considerations/features**

Motivation	✓	This class had very little day to day use of computers in any of their
Enjoyment	✓	work. It was a rare event to be able to use the internet at all, let alone
Excitement	✓	in a numeracy lesson. The animations and unusual "prizes" served as a novelty
Novelty	✓	and acted as a motivational factor.
Engagement	✓	Good level of engagement.
Development of work away from the computer	✓	Some extension sheets were available for those who had both finished the work for the lesson and the online ordering game.
Evidence of learning	✓	The teacher felt that learning had taken place. She re-used some of the examples from earlier on in the term, which had been too difficult and found that the group were better able to deal with them, and more interested in contributing.

(Continued)

Does the use of the internet in this example extend the possibilities for learning beyond what would have been expected if the content of the lesson had been covered in a more traditional way?

The use of the internet, and indeed any ICT solution, was not essential for covering the content of this work. A game of a different nature might have been equally motivating and engaging. The use of a computer did generate interest and excitement, some of which would have been lost if the animation and sound effects had been missing. The ease of availability was a very positive factor for the teacher. Had she been confronted with any slight difficulties she would not have pursued the use of the site and would have found a non-ICT solution to the problem that she had previously identified. It seems very likely that the nature of the activity – being online, animated and fun, was an important factor in the final outcomes, namely improvement in the class's abilities with ordering positive and negative decimal numbers. The class were generally well motivated anyway, but the activity cemented their interest and encouraged the determination amongst most of the children to do well.

Case study 3.3   Find a place in the world

School

One form entry primary school in a socially deprived inner city area.

Teacher

Female with seven years teaching experience before she had taken a long career break when she started a family – recently returned to full-time working.

Class

Year 6 (28 pupils)

Websites

Micros and Primary Education (MAPE): www.mape.org.uk/startower/world/resources/broken.htm
North West Learning Grid (NWLG): www.nwlg.org/pages/resources/mapgames/geog.html
Ambleside Primary School: www.amblesideprimary.com/ambleweb/clickon/index.htmLabel
MAPE: www.mape.org.uk/startower/world/index.htm

Background/Context

The school is located in a socially deprived area, where the children have very limited computer access at home. Fewer than one third of the class have internet access, which is used

(Continued)

(Continued)

almost exclusively for playing games. Over the last years the class made use of the school's computer suite for ICT lessons, following the Qualifications and Curriculum Authority (QCA) schemes of work. This has included a limited amount of internet use. They have also used the classroom computers in year 5 for activities related to both literacy and numeracy topics.

Teacher's prior experience

The class teacher had returned to teaching after some years away. She candidly said that she found teaching very hard work since she returned. Apart from the developments in the curriculum, she had found the organisational elements of the timetable difficult and had struggled to keep up with the expectations for computer use across the curriculum. Her class had been taught by another teacher for weekly ICT lessons during her time for planning and preparation.

In the course of her teaching and at other less formal times she had realised that her class displayed an almost total lack of local, national or international knowledge of cities, countries and places. She had previously used a set of books: "Find a Place in the British Isles" and "Find a Place in the World". It had been a routine in her first teaching post to use these books as a short (10 minute) lesson at the end of the morning session once a week with atlases. When she talked about this casually in the staff room she was directed to two websites known to another teacher. The websites covered the same material as she remembered the books covering, but in a new and interactive way. Despite certain reservations, including her own confidence with the technology, she decided to try using the sites and see how work progressed.

Children's prior knowledge/experience

The children's "general geographical knowledge" was perceived as poor by the teacher. For example, most of the class could not name the river flowing through London, none of them knew the capital city of the USA, and only a very small number could locate their city on a map of the British Isles.

Computer/internet use had been limited to short weekly lessons following the QCA schemes of work and in year 5 and to the use of activities related to literacy and numeracy, particularly literacy tasks for word and sentence level work from literacy sites. Overall the class have much lower than average internet connectivity and use at home than the population at large. (Nationally 57 per cent of households had internet access of some sort in April 2006 [National Statistics, 2006]; for this class the figure is approximately 32 per cent, nine out of 28.)

Resources

The teacher investigated a number of websites:

1. http://www.mape.org.uk/startower/world/resources/broken.htm
    This pieces together the countries of the world in the format of a jigsaw puzzle.
2. http://www.nwlg.org/pages/resources/mapgames/geog.html
    This focuses on UK cities and the world.
3. http://www.amblesideprimary.com/ambleweb/clickon/index.htmLabel
    This site focuses on world and European locations.
4. http://www.mape.org.uk/startower/world/index.htm
    This site focuses on labelling the world – doesn't allow incorrect responses.

She began by using the North West Learning Grid (NWLG) resources (number 2 above) as this was the only one offering activities dealing with UK cities.

(Continued)

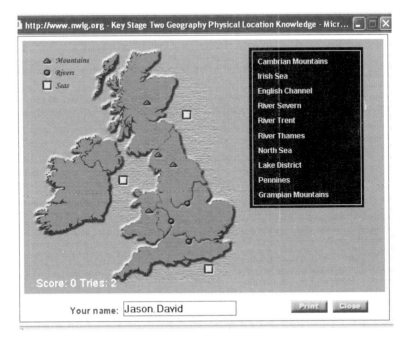

Figure 3.7   **A part completed map-labelling activity**

Format of the work

During the course of a school term each child, working individually, used one of the programs for locating and labelling places on maps on three separate occasions. The first time they worked on an activity relating to cities in the British Isles, the second time on a map of the world, and the third time they were given a wider choice of maps and items to locate – rivers, cities, countries and so on. They were given an atlas to use and were expected to print out and keep the end product each time.

The class were generally very enthusiastic and asked to use the computers at other times, such as break time, wet lunch times and when other work is finished. At times other than the planned times they worked in pairs and small groups, which encouraged discussion, and occasional disagreement, something which the teacher had not planned for.

Near the end of the term, when outdoor games was cancelled owing to bad weather the teacher, very uncharacteristically, took the class to the computer suite and allowed the class to work in pairs on one of the sites.

Response of the children

There was a generally positive response from the class, with a measure of great enthusiasm from some. One or two children reported that they considered it to be boring. There was general agreement that it was better to work with a partner. The teacher had been concerned at the outset that the class might consider the work too simple, or aimed at younger children. This was never an issue.

(Continued)

(Continued)

Views and response of the teacher

The teacher reported that she was amazed and delighted by the quality of the resources, the overall response of the children and especially by the evidence of learning.

Having witnessed the amount of on-task talk generated when the children worked in pairs and groups, the teacher has said that in future she will build this into her planning. In this way she feels that individuals will experience the activities more often during the term and that there will be benefits arising from the discussion and even from disagreements. She still feels however that she would like each child to work alone at least once and print out evidence of their own work.

This activity is something that she believes is very worthwhile. Firstly because it had motivated the class to engage with work in a way that she had not seen before, and secondly because she had seen a vast improvement in the children's knowledge of the country and of the world. She intends to give some time to mini project work on the capital cities. She expects to be able to gather short fact sheets produced by individuals, which can be combined into a whole class booklet, adding a little more value and interest to the work.

Evidence of learning

The teacher wanted to measure in a formal way the increase, or otherwise, in the children's knowledge of national and international places. She did this by designing an assessment in the form of a blank map of the British Isles and a similar one of the world. Certain key cities, countries, oceans and rivers were in need of labels. The children were expected to complete the task without reference to either an atlas or anyone else in the class. Some children managed to label everything correctly. Overall there was a 73 per cent success rate for the British Isles and 88 per cent for the world. This was clear evidence for the teacher that a great deal of learning had taken place. One thought that occurred to her was that she had set the test standard too low, but she was nevertheless pleased with the outcome. She regretted having no definite baseline data with which to make a comparison, but she was certain that for the time and effort expended the learning outcomes were extremely good.

Pedagogical and theoretical considerations

There are, as can be seen in Table 3.5, many characteristically constructivist aspects to the work. This is despite the teacher planning for the children to work alone, and her aim being to increase knowledge and recall.

Does the use of the infrastructure of the internet in this example extend the possibilities for learning beyond what would have been expected if the content of the lesson had been covered in a more traditional way?

The teacher had initially wanted to use books for this work, but it proved impossible for her to locate the resources that she had used previously in another school. Making use of the internet gave far more scope for finding a range and variety of different locations to investigate, and styles of activity to use. The use of online activities allowed for some measure of interactivity – for example, some activities do not allow incorrect answers and so feedback is immediate. This is something difficult to emulate effectively when using books, and a very useful feature for many learners.

(Continued)

Table 3.5 **Characteristics of constructivist learning that might be present in ICT related lessons: Find a place in the world**

Multiple perspectives		
Pupil-directed goals	✓	In a limited way children were able to make decisions relating to their work. An element of choice was included and the children were encouraged to set targets. For example, learn the capital cities of all of the countries in Europe.
Teachers as coaches		
Metacognition	✓	Without input from the teacher some children were attempting to devise methods for remembering. This was because they were well aware that there would be a test of the knowledge acquired at the end of each term.
Learner control	✓	Up to a point. Within the context of having to complete a large number of exercises the children could decide which country, or continent to "visit" next.
Real-world activities and contexts		
Knowledge construction	✓	From a low starting point children were adding to their bank of knowledge, both in an obvious and explicit way (memorising), and in a more subtle way (through exposure and engagement).
Sharing knowledge	✓	When children worked together there was clear exchange of thoughts when suggestions were made and considered.
Reference to what pupils know already	✓	Given that one of the reasons behind this work was the extremely low baseline of knowledge, it would be unusual to be able to refer to pre-existing knowledge, but no matter how a low the starting point, there is always something which can be built upon.
Problem solving	✓	At a simple level, the use of atlases and other reference sources for "finding out".
Explicit thinking about errors and misconceptions	✓	Confusion about shapes of coutries were made explicit. For example the similarity in the shape and orientation of South America, Africa and India were highlighted and discussed between children.
Exploration	✓	On frequent occasions children would spend time perusing the atlases, apparently simply out of interest.
Peer-group learning	✓	When working in pairs this was evident. Also at times there was informal discussion relating to the work.
Alternative viewpoints offered		
Scaffolding	✓	The nature of the activities is such that scaffolding of different types is provided. For example, a list of cities to be placed appropriately on the map. The teacher was able to intervene from time to time to give a little support, but for most of the time the children worked without teacher or adult intervention.
Assessment for learning	✓	The end of term tests were, in part, designed to measure progress, but also to inform the teacher of what kind of steps to take next.
Primary sources of data		

(Continued)

(Continued)

Table 3.6   Find a place in the world: Other considerations/features

Motivation	✓	Again, each of these featured in the execution of the
Enjoyment	✓	activities. Not all children displayed all of them at all
Excitement	✓	times, but the balance was clearly, and in some cases
Novelty	✓	strongly, in a positive direction towards all of them.
Engagement	✓	At times it was clear that both individuals and pairs of children were highly engaged. Evidence of this came at times when the lesson had actually ended but the work continued. At times individuals wanted to, and and sometimes were allowed to, pursue a particular interest further. For example, finding out about the countries in South America who were represented in the football World Cup.
Development of work away from the computer	✓	Although not planned for, there were occasions when interests were followed up away from the computer – the football example above for instance, and on another occasion two girls spent time discovering the home towns of a group of celebrities based on information relating to a reality television programme and an article in a celebrity magazine.
Evidence of learning	✓	Clear from assessment exercise at the end of the term.

Although the teacher had clear memories of children enjoying the use of the books in the past, she agreed that there was, at times, a certain unexpected excitement about using the online activities and an enthusiasm which she put down to the use of the computers.

It would have been possible to undertake similar work without recourse to the internet, but it would have been far more limited and more difficult to organise and resource.

SUMMARY

We are aware that working collaboratively has many advantages, and that much received wisdom suggests that children working together is desirable. The three examples in this chapter of children working alone on internet based activities were deemed by the teachers involved to have led to good learning benefits. All were considered successful and probably better than non-internet alternatives. It would not have been so straightforward to organise and almost certainly not so much fun (leading to increased engagement) if the activities had been of a more "traditional" nature. In part the teachers seemed to think that the motivational power of computer use is one of the reasons for the success of the work.

The teachers in the examples were working in a way that was not entirely as they would work in other contexts. All of them talked about the importance of children working together, and they all recognised the value of talk between children and with adults. However, in these particular cases they had chosen to ask children to work in a more solitary mode. They were able to justify their decisions and they also did not rigorously enforce the stipulation that work should be done alone. They took advantage of opportunities, such as plenaries at the end of lessons to discuss with the classes the work that they had been doing.

(Continued)

If we look at Bruner's four pedagogies we would probably place the teachers in his first category, children as imitative learners, and partly in his second, learning by didactic exposure. If asked specifically what sort of teacher they perceived themselves in terms of Bruner's model, they would not necessarily place themselves wholly in these two categories. This seems to suggest that some teachers will vary the style of the teaching activities that they plan according to the purpose which they have in mind, and the nature of the activity, in these cases found on the internet, which they intend to use. They would probably describe themselves as being towards the child-centred end of the spectrum, even though the activities described here are far more teacher directed and content-centred. It is interesting to note that in general the teachers considered that the activities might have worked better if they had encouraged some measure of collaboration, but in general they would not change the approach if they used the activities again.

To summarise:

- The internet is a source of activities which can be undertaken by individuals working alone, although there are probably more opportunities for collaborative work.
- Lone working has benefits to learning in certain circumstances.
- Children tend towards sharing thoughts, ideas and enjoyment with others, even when asked to work alone.
- Seemingly behaviouristic learning activities can be used to good effect, especially when combined with aspects of socially constructivist learning. For example, sharing ideas and experiences after the event, having access to suitable support, considering cognitive approaches to the undertaking of the activity – "How do you work that out?".
- In the view of the teachers motivation, novelty and animated interaction seem to play an important part in generating fuller engagement than non-computer activities might be expected to, leading to more effective learning.
- Even if teachers are aware of and in agreement with the social constructivist notions of collaboration, they may still choose to ask children to work alone in a more behaviouristic way at particular times for specific purposes.

4   Working Collaboratively

About this chapter

Themes that you will encounter in this chapter:

- children working together
- the value and importance of prior knowledge
- the promotion of social-constructivist learning
- the interactive nature of some internet-mediated activities.

Questions to keep in mind when reading this chapter

- Does the promotion of working collaboratively detract from or add to the learning experiences of the children?
- Would any of the work described here have been better suited to lone working?
- What are the main perceived benefits of collaborative working exemplified in this chapter?
- When is working collaboratively likely to be of most benefit to most learners?
- Were the planned learning outcomes achieved in an effective way, and could they have been achieved better by some other means?

The case studies in this chapter exemplify the ways in which previous experience can be used to good effect and the value of collaborative work. There are examples of some of the collaborative possibilities offered by the use of internet-mediated activities and materials.

The idea of children working together is not a new one. We can trace it back in some form or another to the Plowden Report of 1967 (CACE, 1967), and beyond. There has been confusion at times between the idea of sitting in groups and working independently, and actually working together on shared tasks. The examples here illustrate children working together in a true collaboration towards the accomplishment of both communal and individual targets and end products.

In many classrooms the first use of computers, for any reason, tended to be by pairs or small groups of children. This may have been for sound, social constructivist reasons, but in some cases it was not. Children worked together at the computer as a matter of expediency; there was one computer and 35 children and they all had to have their turn. This led to some teachers realising the potential of some computer activities for generating valuable collaborative experience and to developing new ways of organising the work of their classes. The collaborative use of computer activity has developed to a point where teachers are able to plan specific tasks that require joint effort and cooperation; which lead to the accomplishment of learning aims in an enjoyable and profitable way – as we will see later.

Case study 4.1 Virtual tour of the cabinet war rooms

School

Two form entry junior school in a small North-Midlands town.

Teacher

Female with eight years teaching experience. First year with this age group.

Class

Year 5 (27 Pupils)

Website

Cabinet War Rooms, Imperial War Museum: http://cwr.iwm.org.uk/

Background/Context

As part of the history provision this single form entry urban primary school used some of the QCA study units. In this case, the teacher used study unit 9, "What was it like for children in the Second World War?" (QCA, undated). The virtual visit and tour of the Cabinet War Rooms was in the context of this work, and was planned as a contrast to the focus on the lives of children locally and nationally, which had formed the main core of the work previously covered.

Study unit 9

The purpose of this unit is to help pupils to find out about the effects of the Second World War on children in their local area, nationally and around the world. The effects of war on children today are also considered. The unit expects children to make use of a wide range of sources, including books, video and, if possible, the recollections of people alive at the time. The unit also expects children to be encouraged to consider the reasons for and the results of the war. The list of topics below illustrates the likely progress of the work.

> What was the Second World War? When and where did it take place?
> What was the Blitz?
> Why were children evacuated?
> What was it like to be an evacuee?
> What did people eat during the war?

(Continued)

(Continued)

Figure 4.1   **Example of an introductory page to the virtual war room tour**

In what other ways might the war have affected people?
What were children's experiences of the war?
What was it like to be a child living in this area in the Second World War?
How did the Second World War affect children who lived in this locality?
What has been done since to prevent another world war?
(QCA, undated)

The teacher made a selection of what to cover from the topics listed. The focus was on the lives of children, and there was an element of choice involved. For example at one stage children could decide whether they would find out about food, schools, sport or shopping.

One important resource that the teacher used was the BBC's Children of World War Two website (www.bbc.co.uk./history/ww2children/). This is a major resource that provides information, activity and teacher guidance. The teacher commented that this resource alone would provide enough material to be able to complete the topic. However she did make use of a large set of library books on loan from the county library service and, as we will see, she also made use of the website of the Cabinet War Rooms.

The teacher wanted to add a dimension of political leadership to the work and, since Churchill is one of the iconic figures of the time who played a very important role in the progress of the war, she investigated online sources for finding out about "Churchill's war".

Use of the virtual tour of the Cabinet War Rooms

Use of the virtual tour provided by the Cabinet War Rooms website was planned. The teacher had come across the website by chance when looking for World War Two related materials. The website is affiliated to the Imperial War Museum and is largely of an educational nature.

(Continued)

The Map Room

The Map Room came into use on the very first day that the Cabinet War Rooms were ready. On August 16th 1945 the Map Room lights were finally turned out and the room was left almost exactly as it is today with every map, book, chart, pin and notice left in the same position.

The series of coloured telephones down the centre of the table had flashing lights instead of bells. The three black phones were fitted with scramblers, a device that made the conversation meaningless and just a jumble of noise until it was unscrambled at the other end.

The large map of the world covering the southern wall of the room hangs where it hung for most of the war. It was used to show the position of convoys and the movements of individual warships. There are thousands of tiny dots on map which are pinholes left by all of the different markers.

The Map Room remained open day and night and the chief task of the officers manning this room was to keep track of all relevant information on the progress of the war and display it on maps.

Access to the Map Room was strictly controlled. Only a very few important people were allowed in.

The blackboard was used during the Battle of Britain to keep a record of the numbers of enemy aircraft destroyed each day, and information about British planes around the world.

What was the map room used for?

Who was allowed in the map room?

When did the map room close?

Why do you think there were there so many phones in the map room?

Would you have liked working in the map room?

Figure 4.2   **The map room worksheet (a simplified version of this sheet was produced for the lower ability group to use)**

Not surprisingly an opportunity to advertise the corporate hospitality possibilities – hiring the larger rooms for events – is not missed. This slight commercialisation is acceptable, is not intrusive and does not detract from the value of the site overall.

For this part of the topic work the teacher had booked the school computer suite for an entire afternoon, which would allow the children time to carry out a series of tasks and become familiar with the website and the rooms which it features. Computer use was a feature of all of the lessons but this relied on the use of the three classroom computers and the computers in the shared space allocated to years 4 and 5. It was occasionally possible to use other computers in the library and in the lower school shared area. The computer suite had 15 computers, allowing children to work in pairs.

The teacher planned to have a break from the main focus of the work (notionally the effect of the Second World War on children) after having worked on it for six lessons. This would provide a break from both the style of the work – mainly self-directed and made use of a range of sources to research and report on particular topics, and from the precise nature of the subject matter.

By this stage, the children had experience of a series of lessons, which had introduced the work and then allowed them to consider topics from the list above. As an additional experience

(Continued)

(Continued)

they had also had a visit from the former caretaker of the school who had been an evacuee. As an introduction to looking at Churchill, the teacher had asked the visitor to say what he had known about and thought about Churchill during the war.

To introduce the work the teacher asked the class about who the leaders of the country were at the time of the war. The King was suggested as was Winston Churchill. This was not surprising as they had spent some time working on the topic and the visitor from the previous week had specifically mentioned Churchill, and given his (very positive) view of him as a wartime leader.

This was followed by questions and answers about how to stay safe during the war – in an air-raid shelter, and about how important it was that the country's leader should be protected and still very much in touch with what was going on. For example, he could not go and run the war from another country. It was decided that he would have to be in London, but at the same time kept safe.

At this stage the teacher introduced the class to the website (CWR, undated). The text size was set to "larger" to make reading easier, and the teacher used the big screen and projector to show the whole class what the site contained. She began by showing pictures of some of the rooms, and then went to the "Virtual Tour" link.

For each of the pictures of the different rooms the teacher produced a "paper" copy, which included a copy of the picture, a simplified version of the text and one or two questions (see Figure 4.2). The purpose of the paper copies was to allow the children to see the pictures at a later stage, when they not would be using a computer, but more importantly to provide the information in a different and more accessible way. This would provide more time to consider the text, and allow such things as highlighter pens to be used to help in comprehension and in answering questions.

The virtual tour allows the user to visit any of the rooms that are shown on a small map. In each room it is possible to rotate the "camera" so that a full 360 degree view can be shown. In some of the rooms there are "hot spots"; when the user clicks on a hot spot a window with more information is opened. For example in the detective's room there is a hot spot over the gas mask. When it is clicked a window explaining the need for gas masks and the time when they were first used is opened.

The children were fascinated by the rooms and the lack of luxury, or even basic comfort. One child correctly pointed out that it was, "More like a prison than the boss's place."

Tasks

For each of the main rooms of the site the teacher had prepared a short task. In each case the task related to what could be seen in the room. There was a simple observation-based task followed by a question or two that required a little more thought. For example, in Room 60A there is a typewriter, which it is possible to investigate. The second task for this room asked the children to consider the disadvantages of the typewriter in the room when compared to a modern word processor. The text that accompanies the picture gives some suitable clues to help in the completion of this task. The children made some good suggestions during this task, which were not hinted at in the text.

The tasks were all set out in the form of worksheets and some paper copies were available. The teacher had taken the time to put all of the sheets on a common drive and the class were encouraged to access them, complete them and then save them to their own areas on the computers. They would be printed later and included in a folder with the rest of the work relating to the topic.

Unexpected find

In a part of the site that the teacher had not explored two boys found a set of additional activities, including a game. **"From Dock to Daylight"** invites players to: "Imagine you are

(Continued)

working in the British Government's secret headquarters under Whitehall during the Second World War ... ". Based on the format of "Snakes and Ladders", the game for up to four players, asks questions, the answers to which are all in the text. Explanations are included in the virtual tour of the war rooms or in the room descriptions given on the static part of the site. Once discovered, this game would not go away and became a focus of most of the lessons that followed. If work for the lesson had been finished then the game could be played. It also became a focus for any children allowed to stay in the classroom at break and lunchtimes. The teacher was very pleased with the game, seeing it as a very good way of increasing interest in the topic and of making the children think hard about what they had been doing.

Another game, "Walk in Winston Churchill's Shoes", was of less interest to the class, possibly because it did not include a real element of competition. This game gave a description of an event in Churchill's life and asked the player to select a course of action from a choice of three. The course taken by Churchill was then given. However the few children who did have a go at this reported back to the class and in doing so passed on interesting information about the life of Winston Churchill.

The teacher explained about a good many other resources available from the Churchill Museum website. She considered many of them as too difficult for her class, but would certainly consider amending some of them for future use.

Children's prior knowledge/experience

As we have seen, the use of this online resource came at a point in the term's work following several lessons investigating the topic of the Second World War in which particular topics had been introduced and after the class had listened to a talk from a former evacuee.

The precise nature of leadership had not been considered except in passing when the visitor spoke of the respect that the public had for Churchill at the time. The teacher introduced the lesson with a brief explanation of the leadership arrangements at the time. From questioning it became clear that some of the children in the class had some basic knowledge of Churchill, gleaned from a range of sources, including television, books and elements of their work in school over the preceding weeks. The teacher was able to draw out what was already known and after a short time there seemed to be a shared understanding of the need for a leader who in turn needed the support of others, including military leaders and planners. The need for the safety of the leadership team was also recognised.

As the class had made use of ICT fairly extensively both in the current year and in previous school years, there were no major stumbling blocks concerning the use and familiarity with the school computer room. All of the class were able to log on to the system, find their way to the browser and locate the Cabinet War Rooms site. One or two children were seen to save the address to the "Favourites" list and others were equally familiar with the software. The teacher did recap briefly, and a short demonstration of how to navigate the site was given. Overall the class had ample knowledge and experience to allow them to work efficiently with the technology.

Response of the children

The class were enthusiastic from the outset. This enthusiasm seemed to be a result of being told that they would be working in the computer room. Even though this was not a novelty there was still a discernable edge of excitement at the prospect. This was before the nature of the work was explained.

(Continued)

(Continued)

During the introduction to the lesson and the website the class were attentive and keen to take part. There seemed to be surprise and excitement when some of the features of the site were demonstrated – the panoramic views of the rooms for example. There was a sense of shock when shown the stark simplicity of "The transatlantic telephone room" for examle. In the children's world of highly technological communication possibilities, the idea that world leaders might communicate from a bare room with no windows, and with no obvious computer mediation, just an old fashioned telephone, was both surprising and amusing for most children.

There was a good deal of discussion throughout the afternoon, but this did not detract from the work that the children were asked to complete. They worked well to complete the tasks that had been set.

The afternoon in the computer room was characterised by enjoyment and engagement, with children keen to share their own particular discoveries and follow links and instructions given by others to discover particular corners of the site. As a result of the success of the afternoon and the enthusiasm for more, the teacher was able to arrange subsequent sessions to allow for more investigation to be carried out.

Views and response of the teacher involved

The teacher was pleased that her planning had led to a successful experience for the class. She had organised school visits to places locally (North Midlands), but a visit to the War Rooms and Churchill museum would have been out of the question. It would be too far to travel and too expensive. She considered the visit mediated by the internet as, "An excellent alternative ... almost like being there but without the problems of travel and all that it would mean."

She considered that the experience had added a new and contrasting dimension to the work about children's experiences of the war. The use of the internet acted as an added "attraction" and helped to keep the whole class interested in the topic. The teacher commented that "If we had tried to find out about the war rooms from another source it would not have been so successful. Even a video would not have been so good because with the website the children are in control and can make decisions about what to do next."

Evidence of learning

With this work it was not possible, formally, to measure the learning taking place. The teacher, in the course of discussion and observation, and by means of whole class plenary feedback sessions, was able to form a good idea of what had taken place. She felt that all of the class had gained from the work and learned something new about the topic. Some, who had worked more determinedly and with greater enthusiasm than others, surprised her with the amount of knowledge and information that they had taken in. An unexpected opportunity for informal assessment was presented by the children using the game "Dock to Daylight". By observing groups of children playing the game the teacher was able to note the responses of the children answering the questions.

A side effect of the work was that the teacher felt that certain children had grown in confidence with the use of the technology involved.

(Continued)

Table 4.1   **Characteristics of constructivist learning that might be present in ICT related lessons: Virtual tour of the Cabinet War Rooms**

Multiple perspectives		
Pupil-directed goals	✓	Partially, choosing which room to investigate in detail.
Teachers as coaches	✓	Teacher in the classroom as an enabler.
Metacognition		
Learner control	✓	Choice involved – which room to investigate next; how long to spend in any one location.
Real-world activities and contexts	✓	
Knowledge construction	✓	
Sharing knowledge	✓	
Reference to what pupils know already	✓	Review of previous learning and experience.
Problem solving		
Explicit thinking about errors and misconceptions		
Exploration	✓	
Peer-group learning	✓	
Alternative viewpoints offered		
Scaffolding	✓	Differentiated tasks prepared and appropriate teacher support offered.
Assessment for learning		
Primary sources of data	✓	

Table 4.2   **Virtual tour of the Cabinet War Rooms: Other considerations/features**

Motivation	✓	This work was clearly motivating and enjoyable The use of the internet was not a novelty, but the control of the virtual rooms and the very nature of the resource available was.
Enjoyment	✓	
Excitement	✓	
Novelty	✓	
Engagement	✓	Generally high throughout. Some children were clearly more involved than others.
Development of work away from the computer	✓	Completion of worksheet tasks; preparation of a display.
Evidence of learning	✓	The teacher, based on her conversations, informal observations, plenary feedback and by looking at the progress of the "Dock to Dawn" game, was happy that a good deal of learning had taken pace.

Pedagogical and theoretical considerations

Does the use of the infrastructure of the internet in this example extend the possibilities for learning beyond what would have been expected if the content of the lesson had been covered in a more traditional way?

(Continued)

(Continued)

Since a school visit to London was out of the question for the children in this class, the teacher was of the opinion that an investigation of the facilities for keeping Britain's war leaders safe would not really have been possible without the internet resources offered by the Cabinet War Rooms website. It seems that there is very little material available elsewhere. She was also clear that she thought that the children would not have been nearly so interested and engaged with the idea of a safe and secret "hiding place" had it not been possible to visit the site, make the virtual tour and then explore it alone.

It is possible that certain elements of the work could have been covered and learned in other ways; factual information about the rooms could have been looked at but there would not have been the drive to engage with the site, and to explore and find out more.

The visits to the Cabinet War Rooms site led to one or two unexpected new directions. For example, there is a link on the homepage to "The Flags of the Commonwealth". The link is there because, as we are told, the flags of the Commonwealth are often flown along Horseguards Parade outside the Cabinet War Rooms. The teacher had not intended to make any use of this link, but it generated a great deal of interest when the link was followed because, apart from background information concerning the Commonwealth, the flags of the 53 countries were displayed and as this work coincided with the football World Cup, and Commonwealth countries were playing in the competition, the flags were looked at in detail and discussed at length in the context of football. Space was found to display the flags of the teams involved and a post-it note was attached at the stage where the team left the competition, with a note of the opponents and the score.

The presence of a museum shop was cause for discussion. Some were "For" and some "Against". Some were very enthusiastic about the idea of the shop and gave the view that the shop is often the best part of a visit to a museum or similar place. Others were of the opinion that the shop is simply a way of generating money by the sale of cheap pencils, rubbers and keyrings that always break on the way home. This led to a short discussion in an end of lesson plenary session in which the need to raise money for the museum to survive was balanced against the "cashing in on gullible visitors" effect. The consensus view seemed to be that the shops are interesting and fun a lot of the time, and are also a necessity for many struggling museums. On this point one boy seemed to suggest that it was a matter of duty to buy something, especially if there was no admission charge: "You ought to pay for something otherwise it's not fair on the museum."

Case study 4.2   Exploring places of worship

School

Small rural primary school

Teacher

Female with 22 years teaching experience in a range of schools. Over the last four years, since a whole-school training course, she has developed her use of ICT and most recently her use of the internet.

Class

Mixed Years 1 and 2 (22 pupils)

(Continued)

Website

Hitchams: www.hitchams.suffolk.sch.uk/synagogue/index.htm

Background/Context

The teacher wanted to give a wider experience of places of worship, having visited the local church earlier in the year. The recommendation in the official guidance suggests that children, if possible, should find out about and visit a Christian place of worship and either a similar venue for Hinduism or Judaism. Since it was neither possible nor practicable to visit a synagogue locally, a suitable, virtual alternative was used. (Hitchams, 2006)

Having followed the scheme of work for "What can we learn from visiting a church?" (Unit 1F non-statutory national framework for RE: QCA, 1997–2006), the teacher had arranged a successful visit to an Anglican church and was keen to extend this experience to another setting. For the reasons above an internet-based alternative was found.

The preceding work and the planned work using the internet were both based on the following extract from the non-statutory framework for RE in Key Stage 1:

> During key stage one, pupils should be taught the knowledge, skills and understanding through the following areas of study:
> Religions and beliefs: a) Christianity, and b) Hinduism or Judaism
> And they should have the opportunity and experience of visiting places of worship and focusing on symbols and feelings.

(NC Online, Undated)

Children's prior knowledge/experience

The teacher recognised the value that the work already covered would bring to the new work and at every point in the progress of this project wanted to draw comparisons with the new experience and what the children already knew about places of worship, in particular to the work relating to the visit to the parish church. The teacher also recognised that the class would have other previous experience to contribute to the project. In her class there were no children from religions other than Christianity, but there were some children from other denominations, each of which have different styles of building and differing styles of worship, including symbols and artefacts. Two children attended a Baptist church in the village, one a Methodist church in the nearest town, and one child's family belonged to a new church with no building of their own and an emphasis on worship through music. Of the remaining children in the class about half of them were regular attendees at the parish church Sunday school, a few were irregular attendees and the remainder had no association with any church.

When the class visited the village church earlier in the school year they were helped to learn:

- that the church is a special place for Christians
- about some of the important features of the church building
- about some of the activities that take place in a church
- about the importance of showing respect for other people and their special places and things.

(Continued)

(Continued)

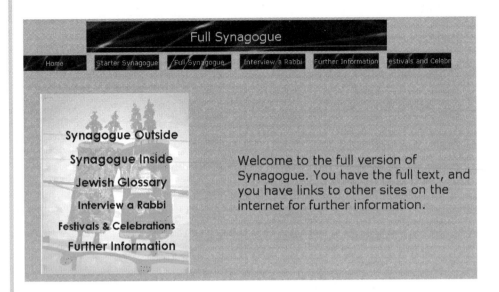

Figure 4.3   **Part of the Virtual Synagogue site**

The teacher made plans to cover all of the above points in the new context of the virtual synagogue.

The class had not previously made use of the internet at school. They had used other ICT for their work, including word processing and simple databases, and also a programmable toy (Roamer). A small number of the children said that they sometimes used the internet at home.

Format of the lessons

To introduce the project the teacher referred to the visit to the local church and encouraged the children to say something about the experience. She then went on to explain that people from other religions have different buildings where they meet and worship. She asked for examples but none were offered. She then turned to the large screen in the room and showed the class the home page of the virtual synagogue. The word in itself was interesting and challenging and the teacher encouraged the class to say it out loud several times to help them to become accustomed to it.

The teacher used the projector and screen to guide the class around the synagogue very slowly and with a good deal of commentary.

The site is designed to have two alternative routes: one entitled "Synagogue Starter" and the other "Synagogue Full". The starter version is simpler, contains less information, is written more simply and has fewer links to other sources of information. For the first look at the site the teacher chose the starter route and showed each page in turn, encouraging the children to follow the words that she read to them and then to make comments or ask questions.

To conclude the first session the teacher asked the children to write a short piece explaining what a synagogue is. The class was divided into three groups for many lessons, according to ability. The most able were asked to write unassisted, but making use of some "helping

(Continued)

words" written on the whiteboard. The middle ability group were given a worksheet in the form of a writing frame which supported them in writing three sentences related to the synagogue. The lowest ability group were supported directly by the teacher, they jointly composed two sentences, which the teacher wrote on a small easel for them to copy.

As we have seen, the site of this virtual tour of a synagogue is at two levels of difficulty, but even at the simplest level it is a little beyond the majority of the children in this mixed age group class without the appropriate support and scaffolding provided by the teacher. This was taken into account in subsequent lessons. The highest ability group were directed to the "Synagogue Full" route and the others to the "Synagogue Starter" route. The teacher accounted for the difference in abilities by providing support materials for the least able, which allowed them to complete the same tasks as the others in the class.

One of the links from this website was for a site dealing with questions about the Jewish faith. This site includes definitions and explanations of terms, and covers all of the important features and tenets of Judaism. However the site is not designed for young children and although the teacher made use of some of the information from this site she did not direct the children towards it.

For the lessons which followed, the teacher, in each case showed the website to the children again and asked them to remember what they had learned about synagogues and Judaism. Then, in pairs, the children were given an investigative task to complete. The task required them to visit the virtual synagogue and navigate to an appropriate place where they could find out about a particular part of the synagogue or about an artefact found there.

Examples

What is a YAD and what is it used for?
What is the CHALLAH?

For each of the items/location the pair of children were asked to produce a large decorated poster and include a picture of the item in question with a short piece of text that could be read out to the class.

The teacher had borrowed a collection of artefacts from the LEA advisory teacher for RE, and so some of the children were able to illustrate their end product with a real item.

The school had limited computer access and so only three groups could use the virtual tour site at a time. This meant that the teacher, or the teaching assistant, could be on hand while the computers were being used. This was important because the site is not aimed at children of this age group and there was need for guidance in places.

The children were encouraged to copy text from the website into a word processor to read out, but importantly, they were also told that they had to include a sentence at the end of the copied text that added to or explained the words copied in some way.

Example of some cut and paste information followed by children's own sentences:

A silver yad is used as a pointer so that the scrolls are not damaged.
A yad is a silver pointer used to follow the words in a Torah scroll as it is being read. The word "yad" in Hebrew means "hand" and a yad ends in a tiny hand with a pointing finger.

Our YAD is 12 centimetres long and it's heavy for a small thing. A YAD is used to not damage scrolls.

(Continued)

(Continued)

The posters, when finished, included hand-drawn pictures supported by pictures copied from the website and word-processed text; they were decorated with patterns, including the Jewish star and other symbols, and were very colourful. Many showed signs of great attention to detail, some were a little more rushed. In the cases where there was an artefact to look at from the resources box, it was photographed with a digital camera and also included in the posters.

The posters, 12 in total, were used to produce a wall display. The artefacts were also displayed on a table nearby with appropriate labels.

Response of the children

From the outset the children were very attentive and contributed well. Some children seemed to have little memory of the visit to the village church, but others recalled details and were able to relate these to the synagogue. The question which came up in the first session (which the teacher could not answer immediately) was to do with christening. The font at the Anglican church is very large and ornate and the vicar had spent a good deal of time talking both about the history of the font and the significance of infant baptism.

The first lesson, in which the teacher led a virtual tour of the synagogue, was characterised by interest and involvement. The children paid attention to the images and to what the teacher read and said. A lot of questions were asked, many of which the teacher chose not to answer in detail, saying that the questioner might want to choose to find out more about the question on their own.

The teacher reported that there was no reluctance about having to get on with the work. She noted that some children were not motivated simply by computer use, and was able to say with some certainty that it had been the content of the work that held the interest of the class.

The overall response of the children to the work was positive, although one or two were only able to go as far as saying that it was: "Alright". In the plenary sessions most of the children were clearly pleased with what they had been doing on the website and eager to talk about what they had learned. When asked, the children all said that they wanted to visit a "real" synagogue.

Views and response of the teacher involved

The teacher was satisfied with the way that the work had gone, and felt that it had been a valuable set of learning activities for the class. The children had obviously taken interest in their work and were clearly proud of the posters that they had produced. She was not able to point to any objective evidence of learning but she was sure that the knowledge and understanding of the topic covered had increased. She felt able to say this because of her involvement with the class during the times when they were working either at the computer or on their posters. Also she was able to note those who responded, or offered to respond, to questions. She was pleased with the level of interest that the work had generated and commented that: "Getting them interested is half the battle ... once they have become interested you can get them to do almost anything ... then you can be fairly sure that they're learning."

Ideally the teacher would have liked to have been able to use a suite of computers for the work, allowing the whole class to work on it at the same time. She felt that this would have helped the organisation of the work and would have led to fewer distractions and made for more manageable plenary sessions.

(Continued)

Pedagogical and theoretical considerations

Evidence of learning

As we have seen, the teacher was not able to log formal details of the learning that had taken place during the weeks of this project, but this is often the case in schools when clear measures are not either expected or possible. Obviously teachers are able to build in assessment, either formal or informal, and in may cases this is done. When questioned about the opportunities for assessment in this project the teacher explained that she was content for the children to be interested and engaged with the work, something that she considered would lead to learning whether or not it was formally measured.

However it was clear that she did make assessments in two other ways. Firstly she made good use of questioning, both with the whole class in plenary sessions and also when speaking to individuals, and secondly she looked at the end products of the work. If asked she would probably say that the process was more important than the end product, which is certainly true in many cases, but it is also true that the finished work in any sort of product gives insight into levels of understanding.

Table 4.3 Characteristics of constructivist learning that might be present in ICT related lessons: Exploring places of worship

Multiple perspectives		
Pupil-directed goals	✓	In a limited way; children were able to make choices about what to pursue.
Teachers as coaches	✓	Appropriate guidance was given, both in terms of carrying out the work and in the use of the technology.
Metacognition		
Learner control	✓	Certain amount of choice was given when choosing which aspects to explore. There was choice in the style and design of the posters.
Real-world activities and contexts	✓	The website portrayed a real synagogue and involved real people and real comments.
Knowledge construction	✓	Clear building of new knowledge on the foundation of what was already known.
Sharing knowledge	✓	In plenary sessions at the end of each lesson, each pair reported back on what they had been doing and what they had found out.
Reference to what pupils know already	✓	As above. Prior knowledge formed the starting point for this work – the teacher stressed this to the class.
Problem solving		
Explicit thinking about errors and misconceptions	✓	Attention was occasionally drawn to "wrong answers" and these were discussed and corrected.
Exploration	✓	
Peer-group learning	✓	
Alternative viewpoints offered		
Scaffolding	✓	Differentiated support, including working with specific children was supplied by the teacher and teaching assistant.
Assessment for learning		
Primary sources of data	✓	Statements included on the website made by members of the synagogue. Artefacts.

(Continued)

Table 4.4   **Exploring places of worship: Other considerations/features**

Motivation	✓	The use of the internet was a clear motivator, as was the visit to a virtual synagogue. The subject matter was not universally motivating however.
Enjoyment	✓	Generally the children did seem to enjoy the work. This was as a result of different aspects of the work: using the internet, working with a partner, seeing and then being able to hold certain artefacts.
Excitement	✓	Initially there was excitement in the build-up to looking around the synagogue. This dropped off a little as the project moved on.
Novelty	✓	There was a limited novelty effect. This specific style of website was new to all of the children and some were clearly very taken by it.
Engagement	✓	For the most part the class worked well and were on task for a great proportion of the time. Certain individuals were clearly fully engaged in their work to the point where they did not want to stop. Others asked to be able to use the site at other times.
Development of work away from the computer	✓	Interest in real artefacts generated by having seen them virtually. Creation of posters.
Evidence of learning	✓	Children were all able to join in a question and answer session exploring the factual content of the project.

Overall the teacher was able to say, despite any concrete evidence, that learning had taken place, and she was able to point to individuals and comment on their individual case. The teacher was obviously well attuned to her class and her view that learning had taken place was accurate.

Does the use of the infrastructure of the internet in this example extend the possibilities for learning beyond what would have been expected if the content of the lesson had been covered in a more traditional way?

As the teacher pointed out, for her it would have been impossible to have covered the content of this project in anything like the amount of detail that was evident, without the resources and activities found on the internet. A visit to a synagogue was not possible, and the available resources – even with the artefacts on loan from the LEA, would not have made up for the experiences of navigating the virtual synagogue and completing the work from the starting point of the internet. In some ways, the teacher considered that access to the synagogue in this way was a little better than actually visiting, because it was possible to re-trace steps, or spend as long as was needed at each different location.

The interest and excitement that the use of the internet produced was, for the teacher, an important factor for the success of the work. She considered that certain children were clearly paying a good deal more attention to their work than they would in other circumstances. For this reason too, the use of the internet had proved to be worthwhile.

Case study 4.3   Key stage 1 music games

School

Small infant school in a suburban setting.

Class

Year 3 (22 pupils)

(Continued)

Teacher

Male with three years experience. Lack of confidence in music teaching.

Website

BBC: www.bbc.co.uk/northernireland/schools/4_11/music/mm/index.shtml

Background/Context

Following the loss of a visiting specialist music teacher, the staff at this small infant school have each taken a different approach to providing music lessons. The teacher of this year 3 class found the BBC (Northern Ireland) site when searching for inspiration, and decided that it might meet his needs and the needs of the class.

Children's prior knowledge/experience

During the previous year the class had one music lesson every other week and had covered a little work on tempo; they had played a selection of clapping games. They had tried composing short pieces in pairs using mainly percussion instruments and they had spent time learning songs, some of which were in the form of a round.

The class had some, but not extensive experience of using computers in their work. For example, they had used simple maths software regularly during the previous and current year, and they had all used the computer for simple writing tasks. As part of a recent art week they had all used a painting program. They had also been involved in an e-mail link project with a school in South Africa.

Website: Musical Mysteries

The Musical Mysteries website has been written to support the Northern Ireland Music curriculum for key stages 1 and 2 (7–11 year olds). However, it is eminently suitable for pupils in England, Wales and Scotland, as well as many other locations in the world. The tasks help children to explore the basic musical concepts of sound, rhythm and mood. The site also provides ample opportunity to practise and develop listening, composing and the skills of musical interpretation.

The teacher's page of the website says that there are links to the curriculum areas of English, science and geography, which there clearly are, but these links are not made explicit and it is the task of the teacher to develop these links if considered appropriate.

The site provides eight separate activities with a series of supporting worksheets that can be downloaded for classroom extension activity or perhaps used for homework. There are four themed units covering:

* sound
* rhythm

(Continued)

(Continued)

Figure 4.4   **The beginning of the Musical Mystery**

- mood
- orchestra.

At the end of the activities there is a quiz. This can be used as an assessment tool and is useful as a summing up exercise for the children.

The website is designed to be like an adventure style game. There is a story involving two main characters who are in search of lost music. Related activities give practice in the main areas of the site's content.

Introduction and progress of the work

The teacher introduced the story element to the whole class and read through the dialogue on the first few "screens". Three characters are introduced – Robbie, Curly (a dog) and Grandpa (a musician), and a story begins to unfold.

The teacher spent time talking about the ideas on the screens, asking questions, re-reading the dialogue and ensuring that all of the children were fully aware of the situation, the nature of the problem, and the idea that they were being asked to help solve the mystery.

Activity one: Seaside Activity

The "Seaside Activity" screen introduces the idea that music has a steady "beat" and the example of a heartbeat, with a demonstration, is given. The class are encouraged to listen to a sample of music and clap in time to the beat – this took some time to get right. The teacher

(Continued)

spent a good deal of time reinforcing the idea of beat (tempo) and let the children explore the beat of a variety of different music (slow and fast), apart from the one example on the screen.

The screen then asks the class to think about walking on a beach and the different sounds that can be heard. The teacher allowed the class to make suggestions (with some prompting):

crunching
splashing
shouting
crashing
crying
laughing
music (radio/tape/CD)
barking
plopping
digging.

The next screen is a jigsaw activity; the teacher read and explained the instructions and demonstrated the game. A selection of jigsaw pieces give a particular sound when the mouse is "rolled-over" and the piece can be dragged to the correct place on a picture above. There are some sounds with a regular beat (galloping, tapping) and some without (aeroplane, wind). If three consecutive errors are made with a particular sound an "answer" is given. When all of the pieces are in place a complete picture is built up and the sounds can be heard again, and discussed, by "rolling over" again.

The teacher demonstrated the process and used a good deal of questioning, allowing the class to make suggestions and give ideas.

The whole-class part of the session ended and the children dispersed in pairs to work through the first part of the story, and complete the jigsaw activity without support. The class were all able to work at the same time as they were timetabled into the school computer suite, comprising of 15 networked computers, a data projector and an interactive electronic whiteboard.

The class were very well prepared for what came next. The teacher had worked through the initial screens and made clear what the children had to do next. The content aspect of the work – recognising the difference between sounds with or without a regular beat, had been introduced and reinforced with reference to both the examples in the story itself, and also by referring to suggestions made by the class. The teacher had spent time to ensure that the class had been introduced to this idea and had the opportunity to relate it to their own experience in a variety of different ways.

The class worked in pairs, taking turns to use the mouse to control the screen. There was a good level of discussion and occasionally evidence of disagreement. The teacher was able to circulate and intervene when necessary, which was not very often. At the end of the lesson the teacher briefly summed-up what had been covered and explained that the class would be able to continue with the story and activities in the next music lesson. This met with general approval.

The following week, again in the computer suite, the teacher recapped on the story so far; questions and answers, moving through the initial screens as a reminder and testing the class's understanding of "beat", which had been the main content area of the previous lesson.

(Continued)

(Continued)

The next phase of the story, with the whole class together, introduced ideas concerning sound. Again the teacher spent a good deal of time preparing the class for what they were to do next.

Activity two: "Sound Story"

This activity takes the form of a book that tells a story based in a circus. The first page is of a circus ring with a variety of acts taking place. The teacher firstly asks about the sounds that the class would be able to hear if they were there and paid specific attention to the idea of beat and tempo. The next page of the book had a short story with particular "sound" words highlighted. The task was to listen to a sound that is activated by rolling the mouse over a ringmaster's hat icon and then dragging the sound to the correct word in the body of the text. The teacher read the story with the class following the words. Each of the highlighted sound words were pointed out. Some of the sounds were difficult for the children to link with a particular word and an amount of trial and error ensued. The teacher encouraged suggestions and explained such things as "fanfare" and "cymbals". The hardest to understand were words such as "tottered" linked to a short piece of music. The teacher helped the children to come to understand the link by asking individuals to demonstrate a "totter", making the experience both active and enjoyable.

Again the class were set to work in pairs going through the activity. The teacher circulated and supported as necessary. In a plenary session, the teacher again went through the sounds and made the correct links to the words in the short story.

The next lessons followed the same pattern as the first two. The teacher recapped and reminded, usually though the use of questions and answers. The next section of the story was read together and the activities to be completed were explained and demonstrated each time.

Activity three: Cave sounds

This activity included finding and listening to different rhythms in the context of an underground cave.

Activity four: Sound patterns

This activity included using a simple on-screen "machine" to compose different sound patterns by dragging and dropping icons related to different sounds.

Activity five: Mood music

After being introduced to the idea that there are certain places where music is played in the background (some shops, dentists) the children are asked to think about how some short extracts of different music make them feel. They are able to choose on-screen an option from: happy, relaxed, funny or frightened. The teacher took time to discuss these options in detail before asking the children to listen to the extracts.

(Continued)

Activity six: Animal match up

This activity provided a virtual CD player on which the children could place different CDs. Each CD played an extract of music relating to one of the animals pictured on a set of CD cases. The task was to match the CD to the correct case.

Activity seven: Orchestra

For this section of the story the activities were slightly different. The orchestra was presented and the different sections highlighted. For each section it was possible to open a separate window giving a short explanation of the section and the instruments which make it up. There is also an option to listen to some of the instruments playing.

After spending some considerable time going through the different sections of the orchestra, and also finding out about the role of the conductor, the teacher set a different style of task, away from the computer. The teacher had taken screen shots of each of the items of information relating to all of the sections and instruments. Back in the classroom these were presented to the children and they were asked to choose one of the sections of the orchestra (family) and write down all of its members. Then they had to decide whether each instrument was a "high" or "low" member of the family. Lastly they were asked to draw a picture of the instrument that they liked best.

Quiz

The short quiz at the end of the series of activities is made up of eight questions. Mostly they relate to items of knowledge relating to instruments and the orchestra, but two are related to the story and ask the children to recall an event. Incorrect answers are pointed out and a second attempt is offered. All of the children managed to score full marks. This is because at each stage an incorrect answer was corrected, often by trial and error. The teacher did not think that this was a difficulty with the quiz. He viewed it as a final opportunity for revision rather than a measure of what had been learned. The children were keen to complete the quiz and treated it as a competition.

Additional website features

The website provides good resources for teachers. There is advice on classroom management, there are lesson plans and for each lesson there is at least one downloadable worksheet. There is also a downloadable certificate of completion which can be printed and presented to each child.

The teacher spent time reading the advice and he also noted the lesson plans. When it came to his own lessons he preferred to "simplify" the arrangements and in most cases used his own lesson plan and relied on a good deal of discussion and interaction, rather than making use of the worksheets. However, he did make use of some of the worksheets as extension activities, both in music lessons and in one case in a literacy lesson.

The site also provides a selection of audio clips relating to and extending each activity, but these were not used.

(Continued)

(Continued)

Response of the children

The children were very positive and very enthusiastic at every stage. There was a certain novelty factor involved in this enthusiasm. This was not because use of the computers was novel, but because the type of use, perceived as a game, was novel. In informal conversation the children were full of praise for the lessons and were keen to talk about both the story and the other content of the site when asked.

Views and response of the teacher involved

From an uncertain start the teacher grew in confidence. By the time the project drew to a close he felt that he was competent, and also that he had learned a lot about the basics of the music content that he had presented to his class.

He had expected some of the children to not be as enthusiastic about the work as others. In reality he was pleased that the children who he had had in mind worked well and clearly enjoyed what they were doing. He felt that the story as a vehicle for the content, and the nature of the activities, which give an impression of playing rather than working, were responsible for this.

The teacher felt that using the computers in the classroom when there were children working on different activities was a little disruptive. He would have liked to use headphones to solve this, but realised that working in pairs might have been difficult, and recognised the value in children working together.

He was unsure about how to make progress following the success of this work. He felt that he would need an equal amount of support in taking the class forward, but was not sure if he would be able to find it. He will certainly use the activities again with another class and will not make any radical changes to the way that he had organised it the first time.

Pedagogical and theoretical considerations

Does the use of the infrastructure of the internet in this example extend the possibilities for learning beyond what would have been expected if the content of the lesson had been covered in a more traditional way?

For this work the answer is "Yes". It would have been possible for a more confident and experienced teacher to cover all of the content of the website by more traditional means, but this would have been a very large preparation task for the teacher. The finding and preparation of the musical extracts in itself would have been very difficult. Having all of the activities ready in one place made the implementation very straightforward. The way the activities were tied together in the form of games embedded in a story made an important difference to the teacher involved. He would not have attempted to cover the content because he would not have had the support that he needed to be able to find, or devise the activities needed to make the work interesting and useful. Even with recourse to the music resources in the school – a collection of CDs and a set of books for children with a teacher's book, he would not have had the confidence to undertake, or the time to prepare, work of this nature, even at a much simpler level.

(Continued)

Table 4.5 **Characteristics of constructivist learning that might be present in ICT related lessons: Key stage 1 music games**

Multiple perspectives		
Pupil-directed goals		
Teachers as coaches	✓	The teacher introduced each section and guided the class through the tasks before they attempted them.
Metacognition		
Learner control	✓	The children were able to work at their own pace and they could choose to return to the beginning of activities and do them more than once if they wanted to. They were given some limited choice at different stages.
Real-world activities and contexts	✓	Not completely, but the children were able to relate to the seaside activity well and to some of the other scenarios to a lesser degree.
Knowledge construction	✓	Yes, this was obvious throughout.
Sharing knowledge	✓	By working in pairs and by feeding back on the work away from the computer, sharing did take place.
Reference to what pupils know already	✓	From a low baseline in most cases. The teacher probed the existing knowledge of the class well and at times referred back to what he knew some of the children were familiar with.
Problem solving	✓	Some of the activities required the application and practise of low level problem solving skills.
Explicit thinking about errors and misconceptions	✓	Some of the activities do not accept incorrect responses. For some children this led to a consideration of the mistake that had been made (especially if an adult was present); for others the solution became a question of trial and error.
Exploration	✓	Within the confines of the activities there is some scope for exploring different options.
Peer-group learning	✓	The whole experience and the way that the teacher worked with the whole class and then had the children working in pairs and making occasional contributions to plenary sessions encouraged peer–peer learning.
Alternative viewpoints offered	✓	In part, sometimes disagreements about the answer were justified by offering an alternative interpretation of, for example, what had been heard.
Scaffolding	✓	Teacher and teaching assistant support was available in the independent sessions. The expectations were different for children of different abilities, and some additional support – word lists and other reminders, were provided.

(Continued)

(Continued)

Table 4.5 **Continued**

Assessment for learning	✓	By the end of the series of lessons the teacher had formed a good picture of the progress made by the class and was able to list suggestions of what he might like to work on next. He was able to identify specific individuals as either having gone beyond what had been expected, and also having failed to make as much progress as expected.
Primary sources of data		

Table 4.6 **Key stage 1 music games: Other considerations/features**

Motivation	✓	At every stage there was good evidence of all of these factors.
Enjoyment	✓	
Excitement	✓	
Novelty	✓	
Engagement	✓	Good evidence of this too. At every stage the teacher noted that there was a very high proportion of on-task working in the class; he reported that there was very little disruption during these sessions.
Development of work away from the computer	✓	Some children spent time looking through a selection of books relating to orchestras in the reading corner. The final activity required work away from the computer. However, the whole project was characterised by most of the work being undertaken at the computer with very little recording expected.
Evidence of learning	✓	As above. The teacher made a comment in his records for each child, noting progress, strengths and weaknesses.

SUMMARY

The work described above is characterised by involvement and engagement. At almost all stages there are examples of children busying themselves with others and taking delight in the use of the resources made available to them.

In all of the studies the teacher was able to capitalise on the children's prior knowledge. With the war rooms work the children brought with them, and this was drawn to their attention, knowledge of the social conditions at the time and

(Continued)

wider knowledge about the progress of the war. Prior knowledge relating to the synagogue project included what had been learned by visiting a local contrasting place of worship. Different members of the class were also able to contribute to a wider pool of knowledge by sharing their personal experiences of their own places of worship. In the music example, the teacher was able to refer back to work from the previous year, which introduced tempo and speed.

Collaboration is also a feature, to greater and lesser degrees, in the three examples and the teachers were convinced that working together brought benefits to the learning experiences of the children. There was no mention from any of the teachers about the possibility that some children might function better alone – Gardner's notion of "intrapersonal intelligence" might suggest that at least some members of a group might be more relaxed and better suited to working in a thoughtful and more introspective way. (Gardner 1993) Sometimes care and sensitivity should be applied and the possibility of allowing some children to work "differently" should be considered.

In terms of Bruner's (1996) pedagogies the teachers here are helping the children to work more as "active constructors" than any of the other three categories. The teachers were planning for and expecting collaboration. There is an expectation of discussion and cooperation, and there is no hint of copying or imitating. The children are seen as knowledgeable. Reference to prior knowledge is included as a part of the experience provided, and the children are given degrees of choice as the work progresses.

To summarise:

- The internet is a source of activities that can be undertaken by individuals working together.
- The benefits of collaborating are clear to the teachers who employ this approach.
- Children tend towards sharing thoughts, ideas and enjoyment with others, even when asked to work alone, and this is something that teachers can capitalise on. We are social beings, for the most part, and discussing and sharing is natural; this can be channelled to good educational effect.
- We must remember that some individuals prefer to work alone and take some steps towards accommodating this. However, some experience of group-working is beneficial to all.

5 Longer Term Projects, Communicating and Problem Solving

About this chapter

Themes that you will encounter in this chapter:

- collaboration and cooperation over great distances, including from country to country
- problem solving and longer term projects
- the setting of an appropriate context for learning, including "starting with the child"
- the use of "ready made" pre-existing internet activities.

Questions to keep in mind when reading this chapter

- What is the value of communicating between countries?
- It what ways can internet-mediated activities provide contexts familiar to children?
- What is the value of using "ready made" internet activities?
- Were the planned learning outcomes achieved in an effective way, and could they have been achieved better by some other means?

The internet is host to a great many sites that provide what are sometimes referred to as "ready made" activities. There is nothing new in teachers using materials and activities that are taken from a reputable source and used exactly as they are found. However, some teachers are wary of using tasks and materials produced by others, who are possibly unknown, and perhaps in another part of the world. (The use of American resources has been considered briefly earlier in this book.) In this chapter we see two examples of teachers using internet-based activities, designed in full by others and used as they are. Both examples are from the United Kingdom, and from well known reputable sources – the BBC, and a local education authority.

Other case studies in this chapter make effective use of the direct communication element of the internet; one in the form of e-mail and the other by means of video-conferencing. The ease with which the communication takes place in these cases synchronously (that is, immediately and in real time) and the other asynchronously (where there is the possibility of not having instant replies, but a time delay of some sort), is something that teachers from previous generations would not have considered possible.

Case study 5.1   Key Stage 1 health education

School

Single form entry rural primary school.

Teacher

Female and in her first teaching post, which she has held for four years.

Class

Year 2 (28 pupils)

Websites

The Welltown website: http://www.welltown.gov.uk/
Wired for Health: www.wiredforhealth.gov.uk/
Rope skipping site Belgium: http://www.rope-skipping.be/
"Jump Rope" tips website from Canada: http://www.saskschools.ca/~gregory/gym/
skiptips.html

Background/Context

The school is close to an army training camp and there are often new pupils arriving mid year who are in need of support in the initial days. The staff were concerned that behaviour at playtimes and lunchtimes had deteriorated and the playground seemed to be a place that most of the children were not enjoying. The large spaces were dominated by ball games – football in particular, and the boys playing the games had no concern for others. This often resulted in angry exchanges and conflict that often continued in the classroom. Teachers were spending time dealing with the problems at the end of playtimes and lunchtimes. The school had a relatively new school council with both a boy and a girl representative from each class. At all of the meetings in the short history of the council, playground facilities had been raised. Some of the older boys had complained, saying that they wanted to play football and some of the younger children, both boys and girls, had complained of the dangers of being hit by a ball or becoming accidentally embroiled in a tussle for the ball.

The school had looked into the possibilities for providing more playground facilities – some benches, a wall to throw balls against, painted markings to encourage other games, and the possibility of extending and segregating the playground to keep the players of boisterous games away from those who would like to do something calmer in relative safety. The school Parent Teacher Association (PTA) had been approached and had agreed that the major fundraising efforts over the foreseeable future should be directed towards these requirements.

When a member of staff attended a training course for personal, social and health education (PSHE) provided by the local authority, their attention was drawn to a case study published on a government website, Wired for Health (Department of Health, undated), about

(Continued)

(Continued)

Figure 5.1   **Welcome to Welltown**

developing games and greater cooperation, leading to fewer problems on the playground. (The site is aimed at helping schools to become healthier places in every sense of the word. Its stated aim is to help schools to become healthy and effective.) This led to an investigation of the Welltown website, and a realisation that materials and resources on valuable topics as well as guidance for teachers, were all readily available. It was decided at a whole staff planning meeting that the materials would be used across the school as a one off and then, if deemed to have been successful, the topics would be integrated into the school PSHE programme and other topics introduced from the website across key stage 1.

The Welltown Website

The activities that make up the Welltown site are aimed at key stage 1 pupils aged 5–7 years. It covers the main areas of PSHE and citizenship as they are set out in the national curriculum, the national framework for PSHE and citizenship and the National Healthy School Standard. (DfES/DoH, 2004)

Information on the site suggests that the activities will work best if explained and discussed beforehand, and this is certainly an important point. The site also suggests that children can work either alone or in small groups.

The Welltown site covers a wide range of health topics, and provides opportunities for discussion and suggestions for further activities. The site is part of a series of Department of Health and Department for Education and Skills websites aimed at teachers and pupils of all ages.

The topics covered by the site are set out in the table below. (The topics initially used by the whole school are underlined.)

(Continued)

Context	Title	Areas covered
Home	Kitchen	Accidents, drugs, alcohol
	Living room	Mental health, the family and relationships
	Shed	Smoking
	Bathroom	Personal hygiene and oral hygiene
School	Our school	Healthy school
	Dining hall	Healthy eating
	Sam (new pupil)	Mental health and relationships
	Playground	Physical activity
Park	Pond	Accidents
	Old chestnut	Mental Health and relationships
	Playground	Physical activity
	Sun	Sun safety
Health Centre	Health conditions	Eczema, head lice, impetigo, asthma, chicken pox, colds and flu, ringworm, warts, gastroenteritis
Road	The car	Accidents
	Road crossing	Accidents
	Am I safe?	Personal safety

We will look in detail at the implementation and progress of the units below in the year 2 class.

Park: Playground
School: Playground; Sam (new pupil)

Figure 5.2   **Games section of the Welltown site**

(Continued)

(Continued)

Children's prior knowledge/experience

As far as the content of this project is concerned, the children had no formal previous experience in considering the ideas with which they were to be confronted, and challenged. Internet use was to be a feature of the work and, again, the class had not used the internet in school. Some of the children had described some minor aspects of internet use from home. All of the class were reasonably familiar with the use of ICT in other areas of their work. Computer use had been a feature of their school work from when they first joined the Reception class.

Some of the children in the class had experienced the feelings and problems associated with "being new", and the teacher planned to capitalise on these experiences.

The teacher did not know very much about the children's experience of playground games, and during the activity had been surprised at the limited knowledge and experience in the class.

Design of the unit of work

As we have seen, the units from the Welltown website were used in this year 2 class in the context of a whole-school initiative aimed at, firstly making the playground a safer and more enjoyable place for everyone, and secondly raising awareness of the difficulties faced by pupils who join the school at odd times through the year and arrive not knowing anyone, often from abroad where at least one of their parents had been stationed with the army.

The teacher chose to work on the playground element of the programme first. This was introduced by looking at facilities in local playgrounds and parks. The teacher explained that under different circumstances she would have taken the class to the village playground and spent time both playing with and finding out about the facilities. During the activity there was not enough adult help available for this trip to take place, and the teacher used a digital video camera to create a virtual visit to the playground instead. This was used as an introduction and digital photographs were used to form part of a display.

Just one session was allocated for work on local facilities and this was followed by four sessions dealing with the school-based elements of the work. The work concerning newcomers was covered in the second half of the term and lasted for another four weekly sessions.

Local play facilities

The teacher chose to use one part of the park area of the Welltown site, namely "Find some ways of keeping fit". She had decided that the ideas introduced in this section would add to the understanding of the work to follow when they looked at the "School playground" area.

The "Find some ways of keeping fit" activity is designed to introduce the health benefits of physical activity, in particular showing the difference between active and sedentary activities. It aims to give children opportunities to experience and to find out:

- the difference between active and inactive
- that it is fun and healthy to be active
- that it is good for your heart to play games and run around
- that when you are active you will feel out of breath, warmer and your heart will beat faster, and that these are good feelings to have.

This work was introduced in one lesson and followed up by the children interacting with the website in pairs at other times in the week following the introductory lesson.

(Continued)

To start the lesson the teacher introduced the class to the idea of the heart beating faster or slower according to different circumstances. She did this in a very practical way by helping the children to find their own heart beat both before and after running once around the playground. Some of the children were able to locate their heartbeat well enough to attempt to count it, but for most this was too difficult. Soon it was well established that carrying out some form of exercise leads to an increase in heart rate. The teacher explained, very simply, the reasons for this and then moved on to look at the website.

At this point the teacher showed a short video, which she had taken of the play facilities at the park close to the school. Most of the children were familiar with the park and were able to talk about visits there and games they had played. One or two related this to the ideas about heart rate, which had been covered earlier.

The site provides a little information about the value of increasing heart rate on a regular basis, and the difference between active and inactive. This was discussed and related to the running that had gone on before. The main activity involved looking at a range of different activities and deciding whether or not they were active. In order to make the choice the children had to click on a moving picture of a heart, beating either quickly or slowly. Appropriate feedback was provided for each choice. By the end of the lesson the class had looked at 10 out of the 19 different activities. The teacher arranged for all of the class to complete this activity with a partner over the next few days using the computers in the classroom. To assist in this she had prepared a sheet for them to complete using the same artwork from the website, which she had been able to copy and paste into her work.

The school playground

The information for teachers on the website tells us that this activity is designed to cover the health benefits of physical activity. It aims to help children to know and understand that:

- it is fun and healthy to be active
- you should be active every day
- there is a wide variety of games you can play
  and also to provide more detailed information on a small number of games.

With the whole class the teacher began by asking what sort of games the children enjoyed playing when they were free to choose and had a lot of space. She asked them to think about two sorts of games, namely, games which need a number of players and games which can be played alone. She also asked them to suggest games that could be considered as active, based on what they had discussed in the previous lesson. The class suggested some for each category and the teacher listed them on the whiteboard.

The teacher had decided to direct the class towards skipping because she wanted to teach some skipping games in PE and introduce the use of ropes at playtimes and lunch times.

With the help of the following series of questions the teacher encouraged the children to contribute their ideas and experiences.

- Which games do you enjoy most?
- Which games do you play at school/away from school?
- Why do we all like playing games?
- Do we learn anything from playing games?
- Are games good for you? [No because you can get hurt; yes it's fun; yes you make friends; yes you get fit.

(Continued)

(Continued)

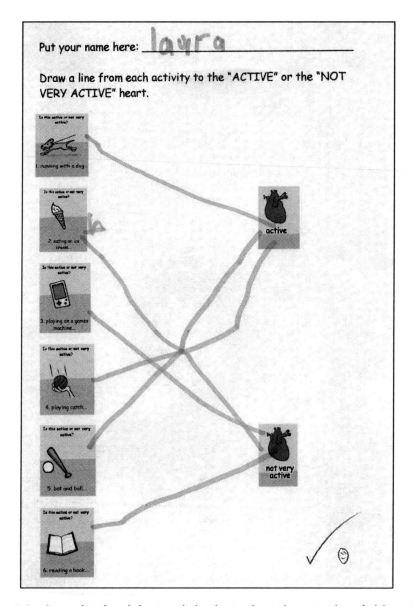

Figure 5.3   **A completed worksheet made by the teacher using artwork copied from the website**

By using simple graphing software and making use of the interactive whiteboard the teacher then constructed a simple bar chart of the various games, and the number of children favouring each one. The bar chart was used the next day as a one-off resource in a numeracy lesson to teach children about how to interpret simple data.

(Continued)

Figure 5.4   **One of the downloadable worksheets from the Welltown site**

In the following session one week later the teacher talked briefly about the long list of games that had been created and then went directly to the Welltown site and found the page relating to playground games.

The initial page includes a short paragraph explaining the fun of games and also the value in terms of health. The five options on the next page offered:

- line games
- circle games
- catching games

(Continued)

(Continued)

- parachute games
- skipping games.

The teacher looked at each of these with the class and asked for comments and experiences relating to each category. There was, for the teacher, a surprisingly limited range of experiences which the class could offer. For example, nobody could comment on or relate to a "catching game", only a very small number of children knew anything about "parachute games". The class seemed to know about circle games and these had been learned either in PE lessons, or at cubs in the village. When it came to the "skipping games" section only about one third of the class said they knew how to skip and only six out of the class of 28 owned a skipping rope.

The text on the skipping page read as follows:

"Skipping is a good game because you can do it on your own or with lots of people. There are lots of rhymes and songs for different skipping games. You can even make up your own."

The teacher talked about skipping games that she had played, and enabled the class to relate skipping to previous work related to active and sedentary games.

The teacher asked for any examples of rhymes, but none were forthcoming. She taught the simple rhyme "Jelly on the plate", which was chanted along with clapping of the simple rhythm.

To finish this session the children wrote out a sentence about the value of skipping and copied the rhyme from the board.

To begin the next session the teacher had found some video clips of different styles of skipping by searching the internet (see below). She showed these to the class.

Video clips of different types of skipping:

www.rope-skipping.be/

www.saskschools.ca/~gregory/gym/skiptips.html

The children were very impressed even though the teacher had been disappointed with what she had found, having hoped for longer clips involving children. Using the school computer suite the class next looked at a local authority website (Lewisham, undated) with some ideas about skipping games. This activity was purely exploratory and the children were encouraged to look at as much as they could and then to comment about what they had found.

In PE lessons over the next two weeks the class were taught new skipping games and rhymes; for many children this was a brand new experience and some found it difficult to skip at all. The teacher arranged the class into approximate "skipping" ability groups and was able to spend time with the least able skippers, helping them to develop at least a measure of skill.

As a result of this activity, skipping ropes were provided (from the PE store room – they had never been used!) and were made available at playtimes and lunchtimes, and proved very popular. Children took to this and soon brought in their own skipping ropes (boys as well as girls) and a playground craze began, which lasted for some considerable time. At the time of writing the skipping rope craze was going on still, but with a little less intensity.

The new pupil

This set of activities is introduced with a story from the Welltown site displayed one page at a time for the class to read and share together. The story covers the first day at a new school for a six-year-old boy, and introduces some of his feelings and emotions. It includes both positive and negative experiences and highlights the feelings of the new pupil and the potential support systems. The story is designed to initiate discussion with pupils about their feelings and those of others.

(Continued)

By using the story as a starting point opportunities to cover aspects of mental health and relationships can be explored and discussed. The website suggests the following topics which can be covered:

- dealing with change
- feelings of fear and insecurity
- feelings of isolation and loneliness
- bullying
- being welcoming and displaying kindness
- building confidence
- taking positive steps for mental health.

The work following on from the starting point of the story was discussion based, attempting to draw on the experiences of the class, feelings of anger and jealousy were talked about. The class were also encouraged to talk about feelings and emotions when they do something out of the ordinary. The approaches taken to making new friends were also considered. One of the aims of the teacher was to introduce the idea of taking positive steps to help avoid upset and unhappiness.

The questions below, taken from the website and based on the story in some cases, formed starting points for class discussions and also for short written tasks.

- How do you feel when you do something or go somewhere new for the first time?
- How did you feel on your first day of school? Have you ever moved to a new area or school?
- How did you feel?
- How do you feel when someone new joins the class?
- What is it like to be left out?
- How do you make new friends?
- How do you feel when you meet a new friend?
- Do you approach people first, or do you wait for them to talk to you?
- Do you like meeting new people or do you prefer to stick to your old friends?
- How would you feel if a new pupil became friendly with your friends, would you be jealous or happy to have someone new in your group?
- Have you ever been bullied, if so, how did it feel?
- Have you ever bullied someone else, if so, how did this make you feel? Why did you do it?
- Would you help someone if you saw them being bullied?
- What could you do to help?
- Do you think it was right for the teacher to tell Mark off?

For most of the sessions on this part of the work the teacher chose to sit the children in a large circle on the carpet. The exception was when they actually read through the story together at the start of each session; for this the children stayed in their seats from where they had a good view of the screen.

The teacher based her discussion sessions on the principles of "Circle time". (Circle time is a well established way of working with children, which encourages them to listen and contribute to discussions as a large group. It can be used as a way of building confidence and enhancing self esteem. There are usually rules in place concerning how to listen, how to be responsive and supportive and when to or not to speak. [See Mosely, 1998]) The children were given clear

(Continued)

(Continued)

instructions and were allowed to speak only if they were holding the toy microphone – the symbolic way of ensuring that one person speaks at a time and that the others listen. This took some time to become established, but the teacher persisted and by the end of the second session the system was working reasonably well.

Session one

The story was read through in the first session and discussed. The story was read again in this session to help the class to be very familiar with it. The teacher treated the reading as a shared reading experience much as the National Literacy Strategy requires. She spent time drawing attention to words, punctuation, style, as well as concentrating on the content of the piece. Children were asked to read short sections aloud. To conclude this session the children were introduced to the worksheet "How I felt", which is downloadable from the Welltown website. The children are presented with seven different symbolically drawn facial expressions each representing one of the following feelings: Sad, scared, excited, bored, angry, happy, worried. Beneath each picture are the words: I felt _____ when _____. With the support of the seven words that are written out at the bottom of the sheet the children have to remember and write down a time when they felt happy, sad, angry and so on. The teacher discussed this activity in detail with the children, offering many ideas and examples. Further support was provided by the teacher listing the words suggested for some of the events by the children on the whiteboard.

Session Two

The story was re-read at the start of this session, and at the start of the next two sessions as well, as a way of reminding the class of the situation that they were considering. The teacher also reviewed the discussion that had taken place and reminded the class of the work that they had completed; she showed some examples of the completed worksheets.

After considering some of the questions from the website that were not used in session one, and allowing discussion to progress, the teacher set an activity for the class. She wanted them, with a partner, to decide on an answer to the question, "What are the three most important things that somebody new to the school should know?" The class were set to work and the teacher spent time with a group of children of lower ability while the others worked in pairs. The noise level was high, but the talk was almost exclusively on the topic set by the teacher, and by the end of the allotted time the different pairs of children had constructed a list and were prepared to share their ideas with the class.

Session Three

Again, the story was re-read. Less time was spent on recapping this time, but the children clearly enjoyed the involvement with the story – knowing the story well often leads to young children wanting to read and read again.

The teacher recapped on the "Three most important things ..." work and then went on to outline the way that a "Buddy system" could work. Essentially a new child would be linked with another child in the class who would agree to be a supportive friend during the new child's early days in the school. The basics of the role were discussed, with ideas contributed by the class. The teacher next asked the class to work in twos and act out a short meeting between a new child and the new "buddy".

(Continued)

Figure 5.5   **A completed downloadable worksheet**

After about five minutes to devise a short scene the class came back together to watch some of the scenes acted out by volunteer pairs. This worked well and then the teacher moved on to describe the next and final element of the work. She explained that the class would be providing some pictures and writing to go on to a web page for new children to look at when they first joined the school. This work would be done during the next session. Everyone would be able to write something for the web page, take some photographs and write short captions for them. The photographs will include sites around the school – hall, classrooms, playground and also each of the adults who work in the school. The idea of producing work for "the internet" seemed to generate a good deal of excitement.

(Continued)

(Continued)

> # We will look after you when you are new.
>
>
>
> "A special buddy can show you where to cross the road."
>
> When you are new at our school the teacher will give you a special "Buddy".
>
> "You can always find your special buddy when you want something or you are scared or worried."
>
> "Your special buddy is your new friend"
>
> "My buddy took me to get my dinner."
>
> "A special buddy can play with you when you are new."
>
> Home

Figure 5.6   **One of the pages from the developing school website. The text was composed by the children**

Session four

In this session the plan was to create a web page of "Info for newcomers". It would include a plan of the school, pictures of staff, and a list of five school rules.

Children made decisions about what to include. The teacher carried out the technicalities. Children took photographs and wrote a sentence for each picture and included a name, a role and a suitable comment.

Children wrote a "Welcome" sentence and ten were included on the page.

"When you're new the teacher will give you a special buddy. You can always find your special buddy when you want something or you are scared or worried."

Response of the children

As is often the case, the children in this year 2 class were very enthusiastic about their work. This topic was no exception. At every stage they were keen to participate and to contribute their experiences and ideas.

(Continued)

Skipping, as we saw above, became the craze of the moment and the demand for the school ropes was high. The lunchtime assistants were briefed and they were able to support some of the group activities that the children were keen to take part in.

The children's response to the second element of the work was different in some ways. There was a reticence at first to take part in discussions but this changed quite soon. Part of this reticence was perhaps a result of the introduction of the circle style approach to class discussion, and the need for the class to become familiar with the rules which applied. The response soon changed and the children became keen to contribute, often with a personal anecdote relating to either being new, or when another child had first arrived. The offering of personal experiences of being new at a school actually became a valuable additional resource when thinking about the experiences of new pupils. Many showed signs of being desperate for somebody new to arrive.

The overall response to all of this PSHE work was positive and there was obvious enjoyment and pride involved in the production of the web page.

Views and response of the teacher

The teacher was very positive about the way that the work had gone. In particular she was pleased with the responses of the children when thinking about new pupils arriving, and trying to understand their feelings, and ways of easing the problems faced by these pupils.

As a relatively new teacher she felt that she was not fully prepared for the teaching of PSHE. She had no recall of any input apart from a lecture in her initial training, and she had not had any opportunities for in-service training since she had taken up her post. The school policy was that if any one member of staff attended a training course they would feedback and make recommendations to the whole staff, and this was the extent of her introduction to teaching PSHE. Over the years of her teaching experience she had not been required to teach in the area, the school had not prioritised it, and this was one of the reasons why PSHE was beginning to have a higher profile in the school. (Another reason was the less than positive comments in an OfSTED report the previous year.) The lack of training and experience in PSHE that this teacher reported meant that she did not have any real confidence in her ability to tackle the subject. She had said that without the detailed support offered by the Welltown website, and the initiative taken by the school, she would not have wanted to take on the work.

Evidence of learning

As with many topics in a range of subject areas it is not always possible to make objective measurements of the learning that has taken place. The teacher did, however, set a short test in the guise of a game to find out if the children had gleaned and were able to recall factual information about exercise and health.

When the aims of a teaching programme are related to attitudinal change, as is the case with a lot of PSHE work, it is difficult for teachers to be reliably confident that the aims have been achieved. Certainly the children might say and report particular views and opinions when asked, but this is not necessarily a clear indication of learning.

It was certainly the view of the teacher that the work had been highly beneficial, and that the children had both learned about and changed their attitudes towards the subject matter involved. From the point of view of an observer it was also reasonably clear that the children's attitudes towards exercise, playground games and the need to help newcomers to integrate and feel a part of the school community as quickly and smoothly as possible were enlightened and positive.

(Continued)

(Continued)

Pedagogical and theoretical considerations

Table 5.1   **Characteristics of constructivist learning that might be present in ICT related lessons: Key stage 1 health education**

Multiple perspectives		
Pupil-directed goals	✓	The production of a "Welcome" web page allowed children to set out ideas and make decisions about what to include.
Teachers as coaches	✓	The teacher acted as a facilitator for the discussions and helped and supported during the writing phases, modelling the sentences for example.
Metacognition	✓	In a limited way children were being asked to consider their feelings, which is not strictly metacognitive in itself, but in some cases may lead to a deeper consideration of thought patterns and processes.
Learner control	✓	Children were partly responsible for decisions that were made.
Real-world activities and contexts	✓	The context was as real as it is possible to get. The children were working in the context of their school and dealing with real events and problems.
Knowledge construction	✓	A gradual building of knowledge and understanding was evident.
Sharing knowledge	✓	During discussions and also when writing for publication on the web page.
Reference to what pupils know already	✓	Reference was often made to prior experience of similar situations.
Problem solving	✓	Real problems were being considered.
Explicit thinking about errors and misconceptions	✓	Yes, in terms of misunderstanding the actions of others.
Exploration	✓	Different ideas and solutions were offered and explored.
Peer-group learning	✓	Some group work and discussion allowed for some measure of learning with peers.
Alternative viewpoints offered	✓	Alternative viewpoints were often a feature of the whole class sessions.
Scaffolding	✓	The teacher was able to make considered interventions at many stages of this work, both in the whole class sessions and also when working with smaller groups. The modelling provided for the written tasks was differentiated in order to allow everyone to succeed.
Assessment for learning	✓	
Primary sources of data	✓	First hand reports about "being new".

Table 5.2   **Key stage 1 health education: Other considerations/features**

Motivation	✓	Very obvious at every stage. In
Enjoyment	✓	particular, when investigating and
Excitement	✓	playing skipping games and when
Novelty	✓	browsing the internet.
Engagement	✓	
Development of work away from the computer	✓	
Evidence of learning	✓	

(Continued)

Does the use of the infrastructure of the internet in this example extend the possibilities for learning beyond what would have been expected if the content of the lesson had been covered in a more traditional way?

It is possible that work of this nature could have been carried out successfully without the use of internet-mediated materials. However, in the case of this specific teacher, who felt ill-equipped to deal with matters that can be sensitive in the sphere of PSHE, it is not likely that she would have dealt with the issues in such depth or with access to the quality of resources made available via the internet and the Welltown website.

Access to short video clips of different types of skipping were a small part of the whole project, but made an important contribution. Without the internet these would not have been available.

It is likely that if the work had been covered in a different, non-internet, manner, the learning and enjoyment may well have been as good, even better, but the teacher considered the internet resources and activities as essential to its success. The children clearly worked hard, motivated and supported by the novel access to quality resources afforded by the Welltown site.

Case study 5.2   Modern foreign languages and video-conferencing

Schools

A two form entry primary school in a middle class, outer city area linked with a local secondary school with "Language College" status.

Teachers

Female with 18 years varied experience; responsibility throughout the school for ICT; female language teacher and language assistant.

Class

Mixed years 5 and 6 (25 pupils)

Websites

N/A

Background/Context

The school is a medium sized primary school in the suburbs of a large city with an industrial heritage. There are three classes of mixed year 5 and 6 with the children in each of these

(Continued)

(Continued)

classes beginning to learn a language during their last two years at primary school. This is undertaken largely through the medium of video-conferencing with a secondary school. The secondary school has the status of "Language College". This means that the pupils who attend the school are given additional language experiences and the profile of languages generally is high; language teaching is relatively well provided for. The school is able to host a number of language assistants from abroad each year to assist in the teaching of what is a wider than usual range of languages. As part of its wider remit to expand the teaching and learning of languages generally, the school has made links with a small number of primary schools and a programme of language learning is underway. The secondary school is also working in conjunction with a local university team who are funded by a European project developing the use of video-conferencing for the teaching of specialist subjects. Currently the classes are taught Spanish and French in alternate years. One of the reasons for this is that the classes are of mixed age groups and each year the children in year 5 move to year 6 and are joined by a new group of year 5 children. This means that by the end of the final year at primary school the children will have been introduced to both French and Spanish. Many of the children transfer to the secondary school and this project is seen as a valuable link between the secondary school and some of its feeder schools, and as a way of easing the transition from primary to secondary school.

Programme for the introduction and development of MFL teaching

- The secondary teacher visits the primary school and meets the class. An introductory lesson takes place and the children are given the details of how the teaching will proceed.
- A plan of the teaching programme is developed based upon the expertise of the specialist language teacher, the primary teacher's knowledge of the children and the possibility of links being made between the topics being covered in the primary school curriculum and the language lessons.
- Resources are prepared by the secondary teacher and shared, usually by e-mail with the primary school.
- Regular phone and e-mail contact is maintained between the two teachers.
- From time to time additional face-to-face lessons are arranged.

Figure 5.7   **View that the teacher has of the remote class that she is teaching**

(Continued)

Figure 5.8   **The view of the teacher that the children have during the lesson**

Format of the lessons

Before each video-conferenced lesson the primary teacher uses a set of routines that have been developed to prepare both the room and the class for the lesson. It is the job of two children to collect the equipment from a store cupboard and connect it to the school network point in the classroom. This is not a technically advanced operation. The camera unit is placed on a work surface at the front of the room facing the area where the class will be sitting, the unit is plugged into the mains adaptor and also into the network point, the microphone connection is checked and the microphone (which is very sensitive and effective) is placed next to the camera unit. The digital projector and the unit are switched on and it is ready for use.

At the same time as the equipment is being made ready the rest of the class work together to move desks and chairs to create an open area facing the camera, with chairs arranged at the back of the space. Behind the chairs is a row of desks that are also used for seating. The effect is to have a tiered seating arrangement that gives the teacher conducting the lesson from the secondary school a good view of the whole class. The blinds are closed to remove the possibility of any glare affecting the view of the remote teacher.

When the class is seated and the equipment ready for use a short introduction to the lesson is given by the primary teacher. The nature of the introduction varies but usually includes a recap of the both the previous lesson and any follow-up work that has been covered since the last lesson. The teacher, for example, may use the visual cues for certain words or ideas that were used in the last lesson and elicit responses from the children. The teacher might ask a few simple questions related to what has been learned previously, and ask the class to repeat together some of the correct responses.

At the appointed time the teacher from the secondary school connects to the primary school and after a short period of dialling and connecting noises, which signal to the class that the lesson is about to begin, the teacher appears on the screen. The procedure for connecting is a simple case of selecting the name of the school to contact and clicking on a "connect" icon. The dialling list is set up in advance.

The teacher greets the class in a well rehearsed way and the class respond accordingly. For language teaching it is common practice to use the target language for as much of the

(Continued)

(Continued)

lesson as possible. In many cases this is possible and the class are taught many of the words and phrases of instruction that will be used regularly: listen; put up your hand; repeat after me. The use of facial expression and gestures is important in language teaching. These are also features of the teaching in the video-conferenced lessons. The teacher at the secondary school reported that she is sometimes inhibited from acting out some of the grander words or expressions, but she makes full use of body signals to encourage understanding. For example, when considering weather it is possible to act out "hot" or "cold" quite effectively whilst sitting in front of a video camera. The image displayed in the primary school is big, and clear, and the actions of the teacher are unmistakable.

The lesson will proceed with a recap of previous work covered, and a review of any tasks which were set. Often the tasks will be to practise a conversation on the topic covered and be prepared to show the teacher. Before beginning any new content the teacher introduces the aims of the lesson in terms of what the children will be able to do by the end. For example:

- You will be able to ask what the weather is like.
- You will know four different weather phrases.
- You will know the difference between the present and the future.

The third aim does seem rather extravagant, especially if it is interpreted in the context of being able to use the present and future tenses in the target language. However, by the end of this particular lesson, in the context of weather and weather forecasting, the class had a reasonable grasp of the way to express today's weather and how to say what the weather would be like the next day. This was not the result of just one lesson, it was a result of a short series of lessons on the topic, as would be expected.

A range of approaches to teaching is used and the expertise of the language teacher is important for the successful progress of the lessons. Questions are asked and answered by individuals, the class repeat words and phrases, they try out certain ideas and constructions with partners and they are generally engaged and involved in a dynamic and lively lesson. When the teacher asks a question with the expectation that an individual will offer an answer, the class are asked either to put up their hands, and the primary teacher nominates a child to answer, or the secondary teacher, being equipped with a class list, asks a specific child to answer – this is not a foolproof method because the teacher does not know the class well enough, especially at first, to know if the child chosen from the list is actually present. However, this is not a big problem and if it should arise another child is soon nominated to supply an answer.

In advance of the lesson there will have been an exchange between the two teachers. Often this is short and conducted by e-mail, sometimes by a phone call. Resources to be used in the lesson are usually sent to the primary school and these are used in a variety of ways. Sometimes to make a display which can be referred to during the teaching or in the follow-up session, sometimes as stimuli during the lesson or afterwards. The resources are often in the form of pictures, with or without words, of possibly single word or phrase flash cards. The primary school teacher is also proactive in supplying resources in the form of posters or artefacts which further support the progress of the lessons.

The teacher conducting the lessons used a selection of video-conferencing specific techniques to add interest and variety to the teaching. For example, she is able to indicate the "loudness" of a response that she would like to the stimulus of a picture or flashcard by holding it either close to the camera or further away. The camera easily re-focuses on whatever it is presented with. Sometimes to increase the pace of a lesson it is possible to show words or pictures very quickly, or to cover different parts of the word or image in order to provoke a response.

(Continued)

For some lessons one of the resident language assistants is able to contribute, or when more experienced, take lessons on their own. This gives variety, which is useful, but more importantly it gives the primary children access to a native speaker, something which is hardly ever available to learners at this stage.

Sometimes it is possible to arrange an extended experience, usually lasting for a whole day. These extended experiences are designed to reinforce and consolidate the learning that has so far taken place. They are also an opportunity for the teacher to see the children in a different context and to get to know them a little better. The language assistants often organise these sessions and undertake the teaching alongside the teachers in the primary school.

The children from the primary school also visit the secondary school and are taught by teachers from both schools. They also make use of language labs at the secondary school. For the year 6 children who will be moving to the secondary school for year 7 these activities form a part of the process of preparation for transition.

Follow-up and preparatory work between each lesson

Between each lesson, which is usually just one week, there are certain additional activities (apart from occasional brief planning contact and the exchange of resources between the teachers) which take place in the primary school. Some are simple routine-like opportunities for practice, such as taking the register in French or Spanish, with the children responding appropriately, or playing a simple guessing game when there is a little time to spare before the end of the day for example. Other activities are part of the planned progression of learning. These activities are such things as completing short written tasks; taking time to revisit the items of spoken language covered in the lesson and talking with a partner with the use of the resources from the lesson that are displayed in the classroom, developing and extending, as well as revising, the vocabulary and constructions that have been introduced; looking at and listening to new vocabulary that will be covered in the next lesson. Occasionally in the lessons the teacher will ask for a progress report of the intervening week's activities; the primary children may on occasion hold up examples of their work, or the camera can be directed towards a display in the classroom.

There is sometimes a need to miss a lesson and so the time between sessions is longer than usual. These cancellations are usually as a result of some activity in one or other of the schools – a day trip, formal testing or exams – not for any technical reason. When a session is missed there is usually additional activity planned to ensure that any momentum that is building up is not lost.

Teacher's prior knowledge and language teaching experience

The primary school teacher has not had specific training for teaching a foreign language. After more than two years involvement with this project she feels that if the need arose she would be able to teach introductory Spanish to primary aged children, but she also said that the video conferenced lessons are so good, and the children respond so well to them that she would prefer them to continue. Other teachers at the school who are less confident with either French or Spanish make it quite clear to the children that they too are in a learning situation. This is clearly the case, but as time passes they are becoming more able to offer support at the same time as managing the lesson from the primary school end of the operation.

(Continued)

(Continued)

Response of the children

The teachers report, and it is clear to observers, that the response of the children involved is overwhelmingly positive. Everything about the manner of the children from the point where they are told that it is time to prepare for a video lesson indicates their enthusiasm. They quickly and efficiently prepare the room and arrange the equipment and themselves without undue fuss. They participate in the introductory phase before the video connection is made with interest and keenness, and they participate in the actual lesson in an equally constructive way. When asked about their views of the lessons the children show that they both enjoy and see the value of what they are experiencing. They are also eager to demonstrate their language knowledge and skills.

Views and response of the teachers involved

The primary school teachers involved also give the impression of enjoying the experience and are clear about the value of the lessons. They say that the children are very well motivated for the lessons and the language that they are learning, and that this motivation and enjoyment has effects across the curriculum and the wider range of activities in the school. The teachers also see the value, on a social and emotional level, of making and extending links across the primary and secondary phase divide.

Initially, when approached to take part in the video-conferencing language teaching, two particular teachers had different responses. Both were a little apprehensive, both interested in taking part, but the teacher who had no particular skill with the language felt that she would not be able to coordinate the lessons well, or support the learning, especially in the follow-up and preparation sessions. She now considers, having taken part in the work for nearly two years, that her position with regard to knowledge of the languages being taught could actually be a strength. Obviously she is no longer in the position of being a complete beginner with either Spanish or French, but her lack of more well developed skills is made explicit to the class and the idea of learning together is emphasised at each stage.

Evidence of learning

The process of assessing the learning that takes place is carried out both formally and informally. During the lessons the primary teacher is able, to a certain extent, to take a step back from the detail of the teaching that is taking place and act more as an observer. She is able to note the responses of individuals and this helps her in targeting support at other times, or indeed developing extension opportunities for those who are able to make greater progress in some way. Other opportunities for assessment come at times when individuals or pairs of children are asked to contribute to a particular activity – to share their exchanges with the class, or recite or repeat phrases or sentences in response to questions or other stimuli. There is also the opportunity to look at any end products that result from any of the written tasks that are set. There are other common activities, for example labelling a large diagram with pre-prepared labels, or even labelling items in the room. All of this adds to the assessment of the learning that is taking place. There is also scope for simple testing and this is used, though only sparingly.

The teachers involved are clear that good quality learning, that is learning which is enjoyable and the content of which is internalised and understood, is taking place in the lessons, both during the video-conferenced lessons and the shorter follow-up sessions. It is also clear

(Continued)

to the observer that the children have learned a good deal and are capable of using what they have learned in both familiar and less familiar situations. When speaking to the children and asking what they have learned they are able to list the topics that they have covered, the constructions they have learned and the vocabulary that they are familiar with, and they readily speak the language, at a rudimentary level, but with a confidence that is often missing from young language learners in secondary schools.

Pedagogical and theoretical considerations

We will consider all of the case studies presented here not only within the simple context of the classroom, but also within the framework of what has been discussed earlier concerning the constructivist approach to learning, and the bearing that this has on pedagogy, and most importantly upon learning.

The prevailing received wisdom concerning learning is that the preferred approach is one based upon constructivist principles. As we have seen, ICT use offers opportunities for this style of learning, as well as other approaches that have been discussed earlier.

Language learning has a distinct pedagogical approach involving a good deal of listening and speaking. In the introductory stages, there is less of an emphasis on writing than is

Table 5.3   Characteristics of constructivist learning that might be present in ICT related lessons: Modern foreign languages and video-conferencing

Multiple perspectives		
Pupil-directed goals		
Teachers as coaches	✓	Teacher in the classroom as an enabler.
Metacognition	✓	Encouragement to think about how to "remember" new words; links to other similar words for example.
Learner control		
Real-world activities and contexts	✓	When the language assistant is involved in the teaching there is an added dimension of reality.
Knowledge construction	✓	Each lesson involves a review of previous learning and the subsequent development of the material covered.
Sharing knowledge	✓	Between the teachers and the children and between the children.
Reference to what pupils know already	✓	Review of previous learning and experience.
Problem solving	✓	This takes place to a limited extent when children are asked to use their newly acquired knowledge and vocabulary in different situations, for different purposes.
Explicit thinking about errors and misconceptions		
Exploration		
Peer-group learning	✓	Partner work to practise and develop language.
Alternative viewpoints offered		
Scaffolding	✓	By the use of specific materials and by careful questioning and encouragement by the range of adults involved.
Assessment for learning	✓	Formative assessment is carried out informally throughout the lesson and has a bearing on the content and direction of the next and future lessons.
Primary sources of data		

(Continued)

(Continued)

Table 5.4   **Modern foreign languages and video-conferencing: Other considerations/ features**

Motivation	✓	There was clear evidence of these features.
Enjoyment	✓	The teacher reported that these features
Excitement	✓	figure highly throughout the year.
Novelty	✓	
Engagement	✓	The lessons observed gave ample evidence of the class being engaged and on-task during the session.
Development of work away from computer	✓	Work is planned for the time between the each video-conferenced lesson.
Evidence of learning	✓	Over time it is clear that good progress is made by the class, with some individuals making exceptional progress.

found in many other subjects studied by children of the same age. The approach taken in language lessons generally, and in the lessons described in this case study are very much within the realm of constructivism, and particularly well aligned with social constructivist approaches to teaching and learning. Collaboration, discussion and a range of different interactions both between and within the whole group, including the adults involved in the sessions – always two teachers, sometimes two teachers and a language assistant, and in some cases with a primary school teaching assistant present who is able to participate in the activities and offer appropriate support.

Does the use of the infrastructure of the internet in this example extend the possibilities for learning beyond what would have been expected if the content of the lesson had been covered in a more traditional way?

The answer to this question at a simple level is, "Yes". Without access to the video-conferencing facilities that were made available it is unlikely that the teaching would have taken place at all. That is to say, the lessons depend entirely on the use of a video-conferencing link between the teacher in the secondary school and the class of primary school children.

Naturally language learning can, and does, take place in primary schools, and it would be possible to achieve the same, or at least comparable results by teaching in a more traditional way. (By "traditional" all that is implied here is teaching without the use of video-conferencing, and not what is sometimes used to described methods for teaching that were prevalent in the past and were heavily teacher centred, and not based, to any great extent, upon constructivist approaches to learning.) The medium of video-conferencing though, in this case, gives the opportunity for language teaching which could not otherwise take place; without access to the video-conferencing equipment, and the link between the two schools, there would be no access to the expertise of the secondary school language specialist, and certainly no access to a native speaker assistant.

NB: The language teaching described here was undertaken as a part of a European funded project "**MuStLearnIT: Using ICT for special subject distance learning in multigrade schools**". (http://mustlearnit.cti.gr)

Case study 5.3   Children publishing their work – sports day on the internet

School

One form entry suburban primary school.

Teacher

Female with three years teaching experience; ICT was a subject specialism in her three year initial training.

Class

Year 6 (24 pupils)

Website

N/A

Background/Context

As part of the planning for the end of the year, this year 6 class teacher decided that she would set up an activity that included the use of a multimedia presentation, digital still photography, digital video photography, sound files, and the internet. She planned to have the children in her class working in pairs to produce a presentation based on the school sports day, including both still and moving pictures and sound files, and upload the finished products as web pages to the school website. (Accessible to parents and school only and protected by a password.) The school had five digital cameras, five hand held digital video cameras and access to other cameras on loan from the LEA ICT support centre.

Teacher's prior knowledge and experience

The teacher in this case study had wide and varied experience of the educational use of ICT. As a student on a three year BA programme she took a specialist ICT route which meant that she studied the use of ICT in educational settings, the design and use of hardware, including a very wide range of peripherals, video production and editing as well as other ICT related modules alongside the standard ICT modules relating to teaching the core and foundation subjects. Before beginning her initial training she had worked for 18 months as an ICT technician in a secondary school. With this very strong background she had been able to make extensive use of ICT across all of her teaching in the three years that she had worked at this school. She was now the school's ICT coordinator and as such had organised after-school staff training sessions on a range of topics decided upon by the staff. Part of her responsibility involved maintaining the school website. At the start of the following academic year she planned to begin a part-time MA in ICT and education.

(Continued)

(Continued)

Children's prior knowledge/experience

The children too had fairly extensive experience in the use of ICT to support their learning. In their current class they had made regular use of word processing, spreadsheets, used PowerPoint, both still and video digital cameras, desktop publishing, and a very wide range of subject-specific software to support literacy, numeracy and some of the foundation subjects. Two of the activities planned for in this project, which the class had no experience of were the use of sound files and the creation of web pages.

Design of the unit of work

The teacher explained that after the end of the statutory tests in year 6 there is often a feeling amongst the pupils that primary school is all over and that they need not work any more. This is not a widespread phenomenon, but in part at least, will be recognisable by many primary teachers. Some have been known to refer to post-SATs year 6 pupils as "demob happy". In order to counter this feeling amongst pupils, many schools like to plan work that is more out of the ordinary, but still relevant to the educational needs of the class. It was for this reason that this project was planned, and also that it was planned with reference to the requirements of the national curriculum for English, as well as for ICT. The aims that the teacher identified were partly related to the national curriculum for ICT, but she also wanted to encourage drafting and revising, and the use of different styles of writing.

The relevant extracts from the programme of study for key stage 2 English (QCA, 1999) are included here:

Composition

1. Pupils should be taught to:
    a. choose form and content to suit a particular purpose
    b. broaden their vocabulary and use it in inventive ways
    c. use language and style that are appropriate to the reader
    d. use and adapt the features of a form of writing, drawing on their reading
    e. use features of layout, presentation and organisation effectively.

    Planning and drafting
2. To develop their writing on paper and on screen, pupils should be taught to:
    a. plan – note and develop initial ideas
    b. draft – develop ideas from the plan into structured written text
    c. revise – change and improve the draft
    d. proofread – check the draft for spelling and punctuation errors, omissions and repetitions
    e. present – prepare a neat, correct and clear final copy
    f. discuss and evaluate their own and others' writing.

The teacher also had other, less formal, aims in mind. She wanted to give opportunities for all of the children to extend their knowledge and skills in the area of ICT. She wanted them to experience a different way of working, which involved increased autonomy and working to a fixed deadline. She also wanted them to enjoy the creative processes involved.

(Continued)

During the time between the end of the key stage 2 statutory tests (SATs) early in the summer term and the school sports' day the teacher planned to revisit, and in one case introduce, all of the software and equipment that would be needed to enable the children, working in pairs, to produce a set of web pages, including sports reports, still and moving images, sound recordings and written content. The plan was to work towards having pages ready and waiting for when the sports' days took place, and then very quickly add new content to the pages and upload them to the school website very soon after the event. The school would have two sports' days, one for the lower and one for the upper school. The class would be divided into two teams, one to cover each of the two events.

The teacher was very keen to encourage independence and to this end was eager not to prescribe the content of the pages. She did however want there to be as much variety as possible and spent time with the class looking at both newspaper and internet news coverage of sporting events. In particular she was keen for them to consider including comments from participants, and to make as much use of different media as possible.

The introductory lessons gave opportunities for the class to remind themselves about many of the skills that they had used over the year. In the computer suite different short tasks were set, including such things as:

- produce a three slide presentation, including pictures that you have taken around the school; add a sound file to give a short commentary
- record a video interview with an imaginary football star about a match he has just played in
- create a web page which has pictures and links to other sites
- scan examples of the school sports' day certificates and create a presentation to display them; add an audio commentary if there is time
- create a web page to provide links to external sites that give information about the events that will be taking place on sports' day.

After all of the above had been practised the final task leading up to the actual day was to create a web page that included all of the background information for the day, and have it ready to import the files – text, pictures and video clips, all produced and created during the afternoon.

For all of the above activities the teacher gave an introduction. In the cases where the children were familiar with the software and the processes involved this was usually a short part of the lesson. In the case of using sound files a more detailed explanation and demonstration was given.

The teacher had arranged to have extra time in the computer suite leading up to the events, and to have exclusive use of the computer suite for the days immediately following the sports' days. The two teams would be given a free hand as to how they worked as long as they were able to meet a set deadline, much in the way that news organisations have deadlines for publications and broadcasts.

By the time the sports' days were approaching, all of the groups had their blank reports prepared. Web pages and multimedia presentations with names such as, "Danny and Steve's Sports Report", were ready for final editing and to be uploaded to the appropriate places on the school website. The teacher had made the necessary preparations to allow the new content to be accessible as soon as possible after the day.

The end products were very good. There were six pages relating to each of the two sports' days and they all included the full range of media and content that the teacher was hoping

(Continued)

(Continued)

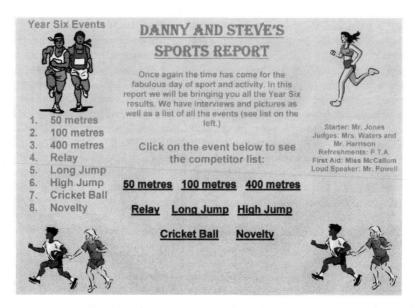

Figure 5.9   **An example web page with text, images and hyperlinks**

for. For some groups there had been occasional technical difficulties and at each stage the teacher was on hand to assist. She also offered herself as a final proofreader to provide a last quality assurance gateway. For much of the time she was not called upon, but as the deadlines approached she was expected to be able to read every group's final copy and solve all of the last minute technical problems. She enlisted the help of one of the school's teaching assistants and two parents as support for the second event, which meant that there was more help available in the last stages of the work.

Response of the children

The class worked reasonably well on this project. They seemed to appreciate the flexibility that they were given, which was, for them, in marked contrast to the working environment of the preceding weeks, which had been highly focused on preparation for the statutory end of key stage tests.

They clearly felt that they were working on something important and this feeling was increased by the fact that they were out and about in the school, contacting and interviewing individuals and video recording almost everything that was even partially relevant to the work in progress. The fact that the end products of their work was destined for an online audience added to the importance of what they were doing. One group clearly considered that their work and subsequent published reports were very important:

Child A: It's got to be good ... the best, 'cos it's for everyone ...
Child B: It's like we're doing it for ... the news ... the telly... if it's no good they'll laugh at us.

(Continued)

Views and response of the teacher

The teacher was concerned at times that the work would not be as good as she wanted it to be. She thought that there was a lot of activity with very little to show for it at times, even describing it as "chaotic", and describing the class as "seeming to work without direction".

At times when she was most concerned about the progress of the work she called the class together and held what she called a "progress meeting". Each group reported back on what they had done so far and what their next plans were. She found this to be a very useful device for refocusing the class, and emphasising the need to be ready for the events and then, later, to be able to meet the deadlines. This technique of injecting urgency is one of the lessons that she said the project had taught her.

She also learned about the difference that a real audience can make to the attitude of the children. She considered this a powerful means of motivating children to take their work seriously and to try very hard.

The end products, the presentations and associated web pages were, in her view, excellent. This view was shared by many others, including the head teacher and many of the parents who were able to comment after looking at the results on the school website.

To organise and, especially, to monitor the work of this project was very time consuming, and at times, very tiring. However, it is something that the teacher considered to be of incredible value and something that she would certainly use again, though perhaps with more time set aside to avoid some of the difficulties that came about as a result of the constraints imposed by the short timescale of the project.

Evidence of learning

In a class debriefing session the teacher asked the question, "What have you learned?" The range of topics covered by the answers (each child was asked to contribute) was very wide. The answers can be divided into three approximate groups: technical, language related and cooperating. There were one or two interesting, but less important responses, such as: "The names of the children in the Reception class." Some responded with answers that showed that they had learned more about the use of specific software and also specific hardware – web page creation software for example, and the use of the digital video cameras. The responses concerning language ranged from the fairly straightforward how to spell "athletics", to one or two relating to more journalistic ideas such as using as many names in a report to, "... make them feel important" and, "Long headlines are rubbish."

There was a good level of agreement when a particular answer struck a chord with the others in the class. The boy who spent a very long time recording sound bites from as many competitors as possible commented that, "... it's ... fun being a reporter." There was a chorus of assent from the rest of children.

When asked about writing for an audience of newspaper readers there was agreement, at least, that this style of writing had to be different, and give as much information as possible in a short space.

The teacher was able to look back at her initial learning objectives, relating to the programmes of study for both ICT and English, and see that they had for the most part been met and in some cases exceeded. In her assessment, she was able to identify learning gains for all of the children across the full range of her objectives.

(Continued)

(Continued)

Pedagogical and theoretical considerations

Table 5.5   **Characteristics of constructivist learning that might be present in ICT related lessons: Children publishing their work**

Multiple perspectives	✓	A range of different styles of report were looked at in the introductory stages.
Pupil-directed goals	✓	Individuals made decisions about how to approach their work – how to gather information, how to present it.
Teachers as coaches	✓	In the use of the technology, and also in the style of writing.
Metacognition		
Learner control	✓	The class dictated most of what went on after the initial input from the teacher. This concerned the teacher a little, when little progress seemed to be being made.
Real-world activities and contexts	✓	
Knowledge construction	✓	
Sharing knowledge	✓	
Reference to what pupils know already	✓	
Problem solving		
Explicit thinking about errors and misconceptions	✓	Proofreading and "reading partners" highlighted certain errors.
Exploration		
Peer-group learning	✓	
Alternative viewpoints offered		
Scaffolding	✓	From the teacher. Use of technology, modelling writing.
Assessment for learning	✓	
Primary sources of data	✓	

Table 5.6   **Children publishing their work: Other considerations/features**

Motivation	✓	Clear throughout.
Enjoyment	✓	
Excitement	✓	
Novelty	✓	
Engagement	✓	
Development of work away from the computer	✓	
Evidence of learning	✓	

Does the use of the infrastructure of the internet in this example extend the possibilities for learning beyond what would have been expected if the content of the lesson had been covered in a more traditional way?

For many years schools have worked on newspaper style reporting and have produced excellent school or class newspapers. Before the time of photocopiers or word processors good quality news sheets were written by hand, or by typewriter, and duplicated on either a

(Continued)

spirit duplicating machine or an ink duplicator. In more recent years some primary schools have produced video footage of news broadcasts created with one camera and with no editing facilities. The distribution has been limited to the number of copies made, or in the case of the video productions, to just one copy. This project has moved forward a very great distance. The means of production has changed almost beyond recognition and the publication, or distribution, has (potentially at least, as the finished web pages were restricted to the school and its associates) become a world wide issue.

The project depended heavily on new technologies and, in the case of publication, the existence of the internet and access to the school's intranet by those with the correct permission.

The teacher's enthusiasm for, and expertise with, the technology involved was the initial driving force behind the project. Certainly the teacher would not have wanted to pursue the work without the eventual publication on the school's intranet. This is not to say that the work could not have taken place without this eventuality, but for this teacher the polished presentations and other features being uploaded and made available was very important. It is not clear that she would have planned work of this nature for the class at this time of the school year without knowing that the final result would be internet access to the end products.

Schools could easily plan to produce news reports and present them in multimedia presentations; they are also able to use digital video technology to film and edit similar material. This would, no doubt, prove interesting and motivating for the children involved, but the extra dimension of knowing that they can sit at home and show their work to family and friends extremely easily was an important factor in the success of this work.

Case Study 5.4   International recipe exchange via e-mail

School

Well-equipped two form entry primary school in a suburb of a large city.

Teacher

Female with 15 years teaching experience: particular interest in and expertise with ICT

Class

Years 5 and 6 (27 pupils)

Websites

Global Leap: www.global-leap.com/
Global Gateway: www.globalgateway,org.uk

Background/Context

Contact with the schools involved was initiated by the UK school and arranged partly via a website managed by the British Council, which encourages international contact between

(Continued)

(Continued)

schools. (British Council, 2006) Through this website schools in France and Spain were contacted. The Spanish school had an existing link with the school in Poland, and the school in Japan was invited to take part as it had been visited by the teacher organising the project as part of a different international project the previous year. The teacher had been involved in a number of similar projects over the last few years and she was very keen to begin work with a new class on a different project.

Teacher's prior knowledge and experience

The teacher was very experienced with the use of ICT across the board. She was the school's ICT coordinator and took a lead in the school through her involvement in a very wide range of ICT use both within the curriculum and as an extra curricular activity. For example, she had made extensive use of video-conferencing to support a range of different curriculum areas, and she organised a "Fantasy Football League" as a regular lunchtime activity.

Children's prior knowledge/experience

The children in the class concerned, as with all of the children at this school, had well developed computer skills and had used ICT extensively across the whole curriculum during their time at the school. They had been part of a video-conferencing project for teaching French and Spanish, and have had e-mail contact with schools in other countries. The school had very good facilities for ICT and the staff were committed to its use. All of the children had the use of a computer at home and most of them had experience of using the internet in their own time. The class's experience with recipes and cooking in school was limited.

Design of the unit of work

The stated aim of the project was:

"To produce an international recipe book with children's favourite recipes. The recipes are to be tested and evaluated by the children who will have the opportunity to include their comments in the book."

The overarching aim was expanded by the addition of six objectives that would be met by the project:

1. For five schools to work together on a joint project in order to promote international awareness.
2. To give children the opportunity to celebrate aspects of their own culture as well as appreciate that of others.
3. To give children the opportunity to learn how to write instructional texts in a realistic context.
4. To allow children to evaluate instructions.
5. To encourage the use of ICT.
6. To increase cooperation between five schools at all levels.

   The organisation of the project was relatively straightforward. The plan was put forward by the UK teacher and agreed upon, with minor alterations, by the partner schools. A timescale was established (see below) and the work began almost immediately.

(Continued)

Phase	Date	Action
Phase 1	9–30 January	Schools to choose recipes, type up and e-mail to lead school in the UK.
Phase 2	30 Jan–10 Feb	UK teacher to send 4–8 recipes to each school to evaluate.
Phase 3	10 Feb–17 Mar	Schools to evaluate recipes and add comments to bottom of recipe document.
Phase 4	17–31 March	UK teacher to collate recipes and produce final version of book.
Phase 5	3 April	Copies of completed recipe book to be distributed to all schools.

The final version of the instructions for participating schools is shown below.

The book will have recipes categorised as follows:

- snacks/starters
- main courses
- desserts
- cakes/breads.

Each school should aim to submit a maximum of two recipes for each category. Each recipe should be typed as an A4 Word document on approximately two thirds of the page, leaving a space at the bottom for evaluation by another school. The ingredients should be in metric measures where possible.

Please see attached example of a finished recipe. Note that the comments from another school will be added in the third phase of the project, so initially the recipes should be sent with an empty space at the bottom.

Schools should decide on how they select the recipes to submit, for example they could all come from one class or they could be chosen by different classes.

When schools receive the recipes that have been allocated to them for evaluation, they should note that it is not essential for a whole class to test them. Small groups could do the evaluation or individuals could try them at home and share their comments with their classmates.

Deciding upon which recipes to include was a matter of discussion and negotiation within the class. The teacher assisted with this process and set some minimal conditions to do with the probable availability of ingredients and the ease of preparation.

The part of the project that required most organisation was the conduct of the trials of the recipes. The UK teacher was keen for full participation by the class and this meant a good deal of care with the use of equipment and the supervision of the young cooks. The school did not have a fully equipped classroom designated as a cooking area, as is the case with all primary schools, but there was a practical room with enough space for small groups to work. This meant that the actual cooking took place over the space of a few days, and it necessitated the use of teaching assistants to ensure that both the groups cooking and the remainder of the class were properly engaged and supervised.

(Continued)

(Continued)

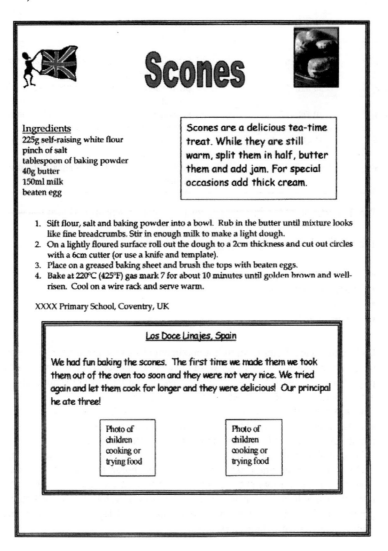

Scones

Ingredients
225g self-raising white flour
pinch of salt
tablespoon of baking powder
40g butter
150ml milk
beaten egg

Scones are a delicious tea-time treat. While they are still warm, split them in half, butter them and add jam. For special occasions add thick cream.

1. Sift flour, salt and baking powder into a bowl. Rub in the butter until mixture looks like fine breadcrumbs. Stir in enough milk to make a light dough.
2. On a lightly floured surface roll out the dough to a 2cm thickness and cut out circles with a 6cm cutter (or use a knife and template).
3. Place on a greased baking sheet and brush the tops with beaten eggs.
4. Bake at 220°C (425°F) gas mark 7 for about 10 minutes until golden brown and well-risen. Cool on a wire rack and serve warm.

XXXX Primary School, Coventry, UK

Los Doce Linajes, Spain

We had fun baking the scones. The first time we made them we took them out of the oven too soon and they were not very nice. We tried again and let them cook for longer and they were delicious! Our principal he ate three!

Photo of children cooking or trying food

Photo of children cooking or trying food

Figure 5.10   One of the recipes from the UK school; evaluated by the Spanish School

Response of the children

The response from the children in the UK was overwhelmingly positive. The teacher did a very good job of encouraging interest by, for example, keeping the class up-to-date with the recipes as they arrived, and talking about the schools and their very different settings. There was also clear excitement in anticipation of the time when the cooking and tasting would take place.

The cooking and subsequent tasting and evaluating was taken very seriously by the children. They readily accepted the need for such things as hand washing, preparing the working area and cleaning up afterwards.

(Continued)

The class were particularly interested in the comments from the other schools relating to the recipes that they had submitted for testing. Some of the children were surprised at the ability of the others to communicate in what seemed like good English, others were able to point out some of the small mistakes in language. They were impressed, nonetheless, with the use of English when it was pointed out that none of them would be able to write in any of the other languages involved.

Views and response of the teachers involved

The teacher was very enthusiastic about this project, which was characteristic of all of her work. She had been involved in many innovative projects making use of ICT and considered the international dimension to the experiences that children have to be an important and integral element of their education.

The teacher considered that setting up the project was a straightforward process, and spoke highly of the facilities of the Global Gateway website (www.globalgateway.org.uk) and the ease with which contacts can be made.

The opportunity for the children to take part in cooking was something that also pleased the teacher. Although there are opportunities, under the heading of "design and technology", for exploring food and cooking, it was not something that was ever tackled at this school. This project allowed for some of the points from the national curriculum for design and technology to be covered, for example, considering and learning about "... safe procedures for food safety and hygiene". (QCA, 1999)

The teacher was very pleased with the response of the children and she was sure that the success of the project was very closely related to the immediacy of the communication. Clearly a project of this nature could have been undertaken without the use of e-mail, but the whole process would have been far more protracted and the possibility of children losing interest would have been obvious.

The end product was also something that the teacher was justifiably proud of. The "International Recipe Book" which resulted from the work was a collection of over 40 recipes, divided into snacks, main courses, desserts and cakes and sweets. The layout of each entry was to a simple template, including the recipe, one or two illustrations, an evaluative comment and photographs of the children involved in the cooking or the tasting. Each entry took up just one page of the book. The introduction was short and to the point and set the context for the recipes and comments that followed. The finished book was colourful, attractive and expertly bound.

In keeping with the teacher's attitude to her work, she felt that it was an extremely worthwhile project to have been involved in and she would certainly repeat the work, or something similar, in future years.

Evidence of learning

When considering the learning that had taken place the teacher initially stressed the enjoyment that the work had generated: "They loved it ... everything about it seemed to be fun. Especially the tasting and testing." It was also possible to identify specific areas of learning associated with the work. Firstly, knowledge of the world, by thinking about the locations of the schools involved, and the differences between the places where the recipes came from and the UK. There was no formal plan for developing this aspect of the work, but it was clear from short times of discussion about the countries that there was interest and an

(Continued)

(Continued)

Table 5.7   **Characteristics of constructivist learning that might be present in ICT related lessons: International recipe exchange via e-mail**

Multiple perspectives		
Pupil-directed goals		
Teachers as coaches	✓	Particularly at the stage of cooking.
Metacognition		
Learner control		
Real-world activities and contexts	✓	Real "around the world" contexts.
Knowledge construction	✓	
Sharing knowledge	✓	Both within the groups for cooking, and with the others involved via e-mail.
Reference to what pupils know already	✓	The new recipes could be related to what was already known, and compared to similar food known to the class.
Problem solving	✓	To a limited extent, especially when ingredients were not obtainable.
Explicit thinking about errors and misconceptions		
Exploration		
Peer-group learning	✓	The groups for cooking worked and shared well together.
Alternative viewpoints offered		
Scaffolding	✓	Template for writing out a recipe simply and concisely was provided. Varying levels of support were given during the cooking.
Assessment for learning		
Primary sources of data	✓	The recipes and the ingredients.

Table 5.8   **International recipe exchange via e-mail: Other considerations/features**

Motivation	✓	The class were generally well motivated and enjoyed the work.
Enjoyment	✓	
Excitement	✓	They became more excited at the time for tasting.
Novelty	✓	It was a novelty at two levels, firstly the communication with other far off schools, and also actually cooking at school.
Engagement	✓	High throughout.
Development of work away from the computer	✓	The cooking and tasting.
Evidence of learning	✓	Yes, though not formal assessment.

increase in knowledge. Secondly, knowledge concerning food in different countries and insight into cultural differences. The third category of learning involved the practice and learning of a range of skills associated with cooking. These were in many cases at a fairly low level of difficulty, but for many of the children involved it was the first time that they had been introduced to them. The skills included such things as: using a sharp knife to cut ingredients, using measuring equipment, peeling potatoes, and even in some cases using a can opener. Some of the vocabulary associated with cooking was also introduced and in some cases discussed: blend, dice, garnish. Some ingredients were also new to some of the class: tofu, asparagus.

The end products, both the specific item of food and the evaluations, also showed evidence of learning, practising skills of food preparation and of writing concisely for a particular audience.

(Continued)

Does the use of the internet in this example extend the possibilities for learning beyond what would have been expected if the content of the lesson had been covered in a more traditional way?

As with other projects which rely on contact with others, it is possible that this project might have taken place without access to rapid electronic communication. However the teacher is certain that this project would not have been viable without e-mail. Using other forms of communication would have detracted so much from the immediacy, excitement and interest, which was contributed to by the very swift responses, that the teacher considered the project would not have been worth pursuing except by e-mail.

The possibilities for exchange and communication added an important dimension to the work. The teacher said that, "It was knowing that the recipes came from real people in real schools that made a big difference to the class's interest ... we could have got recipes from a book, but it wouldn't have been so good."

Another motivator was the food preparation and most importantly the food tasting. Although many of the children had travelled to France and Spain, they were not able to comment in detail on any of the local food. Being able to make, taste and comment upon, knowing that the comments were directed at a real audience, gave the work an added importance and authenticity, which in turn contributed to its success.

Case study 5.5   Using a webquest

School

Semi-rural one form entry primary school.

Teacher

Male with two years experience.

Class

Year 5 (26 pupils)

Websites

Webquest UK: www.webquestuk.org.uk/
Kent National Grid for Learning – history section: www.kented.org.uk/ngfl/subjects/history/webenquiry/greeks/index.html

Background/Context

Before describing the progress of this project it is important to outline the basic structure and use of a webquest. A webquest is an online resource that presents information, tasks and links for children to use when working on a particular topic.

(Continued)

(Continued)

A webquest can be of any size, one or two pages, or a set of many more, and consists of an introductory web page that sets out the structure, content and activity. Children are set to work on a particular project, given information, tasks and links to further supporting information and expected, with appropriate teacher support, to fulfill what is asked of them. Webquests vary greatly in their style and intentions, some are expansive and designed to provide the backbone of the work in a particular topic for a whole school term; others are less grand and serve to introduce a topic, to reinforce other activities or to act as a conclusion to work carried out.

Webquests are built around a central structure, which consists of a series of headings. For each heading there is an expectation that certain information will be given and that certain tasks and related learning activities will be set, which will be completed by the children following the quest. The Webquest UK website says:

> All webquests follow a clearly defined structure. Some uses of the internet stop at the point where pupils locate web resources. Webquests require pupils to reconstruct their learning into a report or presentation of their own.
> (Webquest UK, undated)

This clearly indicates an approach to learning activities that is wholly in line with constructivist learning theory.

Webquests can differ widely from each other. There is no fixed and inflexible approach that must be taken, and there are no rules for their creation. There is however a structure that all webquests follow. The structure is not a limiting factor and there is scope for developing activities in many different ways. If account is taken of the context of the work, attention is given to pre-existing knowledge, and the social constructivist notions of collaboration and co-operation are put into practice, the power of the webquest to promote enjoyable and effective learning can be great.

The headings in the structure of a webquest are:

- A title – The name of the webquest. This can be something designed to inspire interest, or a simple description of the content of the quest.
- An introduction – This is often short and sets the scene for what is to come.
- Process – What to do. This section sets out the task or tasks which are to be completed. Often a good deal of guidance is given and suggestions for how to complete the tasks.
- Resources – This section can vary enormously. There can be documents, diagrams, photographs, maps, sound files, video clips, access to primary sources. In short, anything which will be needed to complete the tasks. In most cases the resources are embedded within the structure of the webquest, but there are also opportunities for links to be made to other locations on the internet where access can be made to sources of information needed to complete the tasks.
- Evaluation – In this section the success criteria are made very clear to the children. They are told what it is that they have to do in order to have completed the quest successfully. This approach to teaching and learning is gaining a strong foothold in schools. If children are clear about what is expected of them it is far more likely that they will be able to achieve it. In many classrooms throughout the country teachers write the learning objective on the board at the beginning of lessons and draw the attention of the class to it. In this way, it is thought, children are better able to understand what it is they are doing and to what end.

The Greek Worship webquest

This webquest is found on the website of the Kent National Grid for Learning (NGfL www.kented.org.uk). It is an example of what Dodge (1997) has named a "short term

(Continued)

Figure 5.11   **Opening page of the Greek Worship webquest**

webquest". It is designed to be completed in a relatively short space of time, probably no more than two or three lessons. The teacher actually allowed a little longer than this, aiming to work on it for half of a term. To supplement the work from the webquest he had planned for groups of children to design and make posters to advertise particular gods and religious events from the time, which would, to a certain extent, bring together the work covered online.

The webquest is designed for year 5 children following the history Unit 14 "Who were the Ancient Greeks?" (DfES/QCA, 1997–2006) The activities centre around Ancient Greek religion and help the children investigate who the Ancient Greeks worshipped and why.

A series of questions is presented on a web page. After each question is a link to a web resource where the children are able to find information that will help them write answers to the questions.

Not all the answers are directly contained in the resources. The children are encouraged, both by the suggestions on the site, and by the teacher, to infer answers from the historical sources presented. Some questions ask the children for their opinions and for explanations.

There are two printable sheets to help the children record their findings. They are to be given to the children before they begin the enquiry.

There is a page for teachers associated with the webquest that gives a clear picture of the way that it links to the national curriculum for history, and the way in which the quest has been planned and should be used.

The teachers' page was found at: www.kented.org.uk/ngfl/subjects/history/webenquiry/greeks/index.html

(Continued)

(Continued)

Teacher's prior knowledge and experience

The teacher had been introduced to webquests as part of his initial training. He had completed an assignment that involved evaluating a "ready made" webquest, and planning a webquest of his own. He had been impressed by the potential of this style of work and had been looking for an opportunity to use one with his class. This particular history topic had given him the opportunity.

In his teaching he uses the internet occasionally, for example he has shown images of a Caribbean island in the context of a geography topic, and he has used some online activities in literacy lessons. He is a competent and confident user of ICT, both in his professional and personal life.

Children's prior knowledge/experience

The children have used ICT throughout their time at this primary school, in the earlier years this was not straightforward as the facilities were poor. Three years ago a new room was made available for a computer suite and since then they have been able to use the room on a weekly basis. The class were generally competent with the applications that were used and they were still enthusiastic about the use of the "new" computer room. All of the children had access, of one sort or another, to a computer at home and occasionally they were able to find information from the internet to support their work in school.

Using the "Who Did the Greeks Worship and Why?" webquest

The children were introduced to the webquest, after a brief question and answer session about the Ancient Greeks. The only points of reference that the teacher was able to establish were to do with the Olympic Games and vague recollections, based on films such as "Jason and the Argonauts". Two children had visited Greece for a holiday, but were not able to contribute anything related to Greece in ancient times.

It was explained to the class that in some cases it would be necessary to read quite a lot of information in order to be able to answer the questions. The teacher was keen to help to develop skills of using information effectively and also keen to avoid any hint of simply copying text from the page of information to the answer sheet. To this end he suggested two things for the class to try. Firstly, that they should print out the information and then use a highlighter pen to show anything on the page that was relevant to the answering of the question. Secondly, use the highlighted sentences to write an answer, including all of the points that actually answer the question.

There are two routes through the webquest and the teacher set one group of children, about half of the class, along one route, "Temples and sacred places", and the remainder of the class along the route following "Ancient Greek gods and goddesses". He asked the lower ability children to follow the "Gods and goddesses" route as it was a more straightforward set of tasks and the reading requirement both less challenging and shorter. The more able group were asked to work on the "Temples and sacred places" route and expected to have at least started to work on the second route before the end of the project. What actually happened was that all of the class worked on both parts of the webquest. The more able children found the first section reasonably straightforward and the second section a little easier, while the least able in the second group struggled a little and were given appropriate support (additional teacher input and simplified texts) with the "Gods and goddesses" section and did not attempt the other section.

(Continued)

Response of the children

The children were attentive during the introduction to the webquest, and asked a lot of questions. They were enthusiastic and keen to begin their work. To begin with they worked reasonably well, the more able children concentrated well and completed a lot of work in the first session. By the time of the second session the interest of the class seemed to fall off a little, although a group of children working on the "Temples and sacred places" section continued to work very hard. The remainder of the class needed to be reminded to get on and were in need of more support than the teacher had anticipated.

When asked specifically about what they thought about the webquest work, the majority of the children spoken to said that they liked the work, that they liked the idea of a webquest and that it had been enjoyable. One or two spoke honestly about the difficulties that they had found with the work, agreeing that it was: "Okay, if the teacher was there to help."

One child was so enthusiastic about webquests that he suggested that he should be allowed to create a webquest for the rest of the class to use, an idea which seemed to interest the teacher.

Views and response of the teacher

Overall the teacher considered that this particular webquest was not wholly suitable for his class, especially the lower achievers. He considered that it was at the right level for the higher achievers and this group benefited from the work. He was disappointed that so much of his time was needed to support the least able children, despite having made provision for their support with customised materials.

Some of the texts that the links referenced were too difficult for some of the children to deal with, for example "The Acropolis of Athens". The teacher spent some time simplifying the text of one or two of them and giving printed copies to some groups.

He was surprised to find that some of the links did not work as they were supposed to, even though they had worked when he first looked at the site. In all cases the user was automatically redirected to the new location of the page.

He considered this, his first use of a webquest, to be an important learning experience. He realised that to be fully successful a webquest must cater for all of the needs of all of the class. In particular there must be adequate differentiation built in to the tasks.

As part of his professional development targets, agreed with his head teacher, he will work on the development of a webquest of his own for use with the class that he will have next year. He has come to the view that webquests are valuable tools, likely to lead to enthusiasm and to effective learning, and he is keen to develop their use, but he has also arrived at the conclusion that the best webquests will not be "off the peg" as he put it, but "made to measure". By this he meant that the best webquests are probably those created for a specific class by a teacher who knows them well, and is able to cater fully for their needs.

Evidence of learning

In the final session of this project, when the last tasks were being completed and the posters being finalised, the teacher managed to speak to all of the children in the class in order to be able to make informal assessments of the learning outcomes of the work. He wanted to establish if individual children knew more by the end of the project than at the beginning – given the low base line of knowledge, this should not have been difficult to achieve.

(Continued)

(Continued)

He also wanted to talk about the processes that they had been through in finding information and then using it to answer the questions. He asked specifically about how they had managed to use the fairly long texts to help in the answering of the question.

It was clear that the children had learned factual information relating to the topic. They were able to talk about particular aspects of the work, though sometimes at a simple level, using correct terms and names for example.

When talking about working with the information some of the children explained and showed examples of the use of printed sheets and highlighting, and some agreed that this approach had been useful. Others were less well able to explain how they had worked.

In looking at the written responses it was clear in a minority of cases that some words had been copied directly, but it did also seem that many of the children had been able to compile answers to the questions by combining elements from different places in the text, and in one or two cases from different sources.

Pedagogical and theoretical considerations

Table 5.9   **Characteristics of constructivist learning that might be present in ICT related lessons: Using a webquest**

Multiple perspectives		
Pupil-directed goals		
Teachers as coaches	✓	Yes, in how to use the webquest and in how to deal with the long texts.
Metacognition	✓	The teacher hinted at "a way of working" (highlighting sentences) and tried to get the class to think about how best to deal with texts when looking for specific information.
Learner control	✓	Partly; individuals were able to make choices about what to do next, and when to work away from the computers.
Real-world activities and contexts		
Knowledge construction	✓	From a low starting point, knowledge was built up as the tasks were completed.
Sharing knowledge	✓	The posters allowed for a little passing on of what had been covered by different groups.
Reference to what pupils know already	✓	The teacher began by encouraging the class to think hard about what they already knew of the time. At the time of the activity, it was very little.
Problem solving		
Explicit thinking about errors and misconceptions		
Exploration	✓	Time was allowed for exploring the webquest and for some of the class, who asked specifically, outside of the confines of the webquest, using Google for Kids to search out more information.
Peer-group learning		
Alternative viewpoints offered	✓	There were some minor disagreements on factual matters, these were mainly owing to misunderstanding of one sort or another.
Scaffolding	✓	Teacher support was a feature of the project, especially for the least able; customised materials were also produced at a more appropriate level for some of the class – more of this may have been needed.

(Continued)

Table 5.9   **Continued**

Assessment for learning	✓	Based on his conversations with individuals the teacher formed a clear idea of how he could develop improved information handling skills. He went on to plan a series of lessons based on finding information in texts and how to make good use of it.
Primary sources of data		

Table 5.10   **Using a webquest: Other considerations/features**

Motivation	✓	The use of a webquest was certainly
Enjoyment	✓	a motivator for all of the class initially,
Excitement	✓	and later for the most able in particular.
Novelty	✓	There was a measure of enjoyment, excitement and novelty, but this decreased as the project moved on, especially for the least able.
Engagement	✓	Again, the most able engaged well, the least able less so.
Development of work away from the computer	✓	There was some reference to other sources of information. The posters were created away from the computers, and based entirely on what had been learned.
Evidence of learning	✓	The teacher felt satisfied that the class knew more about the Ancient Greeks' religion by the end of the project, and he also felt that some progress had been made with using information from texts.

Does the use of the infrastructure of the internet in this example extend the possibilities for learning beyond what would have been expected if the content of the lesson had been covered in a more traditional way?

By definition, a webquest can only exist within the infrastructure of the internet. As with many internet-mediated activities, it is possible that they could, most likely in a modified form, have been undertaken in other "non-internet" ways.

In the case of the webquest in this study, it would have been possible to organise for the work to be carried out differently, but certainly not easy to do so. To gather together the resources that were available through the webquest and to have them simultaneously available to, potentially, 13 pairs of children would not be possible. In the school in question the resources for teaching about the Ancient Greeks were limited to entries in a set of encyclopaedias, and to four posters showing scenes from Ancient Greek life. It would have been possible to acquire resources, some purchased, and perhaps some on loan, but the breadth and quality of what was integrated into the webquest, as well as those items accessed by a few children separately, could not have been matched.

It is also the case that, despite a little flagging of interest from some of the class, the motivation and engagement amongst the class was generally high. The teacher's final view of the work was that it was beneficial, it worked on many levels but could have been more successful with more variation and differentiation. He also considered that it would not, at that time, have been possible for him to carry out similar work in any other way.

SUMMARY

As a means for communicating the internet surpasses everything that has gone before. With the exception of the telephone, which has never really been exploited as an educational tool, there has never been a means of immediate long distance communication available for educational purposes. Now that the technology has developed beyond its infancy in the 1990s there are a range of opportunities being developed by creative teachers and encouraged by some sections of industry and commerce – the "Ask an Expert" service provided by some national and multinational companies for example. There are also numerous sites offering "chat" and other contact for what are clearly educational purposes – the Homework Elephant for example, or the BBC Bite Size pages provided for exam help and revision at all levels.

The internet as a medium for the publication of children's work has until recently, perhaps, been overlooked. There have been some notable examples of high profile school websites containing children's work, but it is now becoming more common for schools to put examples of children's work on the school site and in some cases whole projects are posted, projects such as the example of sports reporting here. The internet provides a real location of work with a range of different audiences. For example, work can be posted, with permission, to specific sites for the purpose of showcasing school work; some museums encourage schools to submit examples of work, similarly with art galleries; local newspapers sometimes have sites where real reports on real events written by school children are placed. There are many opportunities for publishing on a wide stage and there are also possibilities for local publication, as in the example here, when the work was published on a restricted access section of the school website.

In terms of the pedagogy seen in the five case studies in this chapter, we have seen even the youngest of the children, in the PSHE project, being encouraged to work independently, being offered the opportunity to make choices, and being encouraged to collaborate at a high level – especially in the sports reporting work. The teachers responsible for planning this work made very good use of the internet, both as a source of material and a communication tool, and also as a location for publication, and planned for the children to work in a range of constructivist and socially constructivist ways. At each stage in these particular projects, and in many of the others reported in this book, children have been provided with opportunities to discuss and communicate. The foreign language teaching example is perhaps a slightly different type of discussion and communication, but within the distinctive pedagogy of foreign languages teaching, the internet has served to stimulate and develop skills and understanding which would not have been possible in the context of the school in question.

To summarise:

- The capacity of the internet to mediate high quality communication of different types (in particular, e-mail, video-conferencing, synchronous and asynchronous) has made it possible to develop projects that are simple and yet very effective, and allow in the cases described here for teaching to take place that would not otherwise have been possible.
- The internet is a source of project work, such as webquests, created by experienced teachers and often designed to meet specific curriculum requirements.
- Many internet-based projects allow for a measure of choice and autonomy, which suits the methods and pedagogy of many teachers, and which is also appreciated by many children.
- The internet can be a source of activity and other material that allows for certain work to be carried out, which would otherwise prove difficult to complete.
- Internet-based activities are usually created with specific pedagogical considerations in mind. The medium of the internet can be used equally to promote behaviourist or constructivist learning – content can be approached in different ways in exactly the same way as a teacher might choose an approach to teaching without the use of ICT or the internet. The final choice of pedagogy rests with the teacher.
- Pupils are interested in and, in many cases highly motivated by, internet mediated activity and communication seems to rate more highly with many pupils than other internet uses.

6 End Word: Effective Teaching with the Internet

One of the intentions of this book is to explore some of the issues surrounding the increasing use of the internet in schools. In an attempt to do this, some background theory has been discussed as has the current state of thinking about pedagogy as it relates to what teachers perceive as their role in developing learning mediated by internet-based resources. Another important issue that has been considered is the validity, integrity, reliability, trustworthiness, call it what you may, and the real educational value of material held on the internet and accessed for use in classrooms. This particular issue, which calls for the careful evaluation of anything to be used by pupils, is of particular importance since the internet is an unregulated environment and resources of both very great value can at times sit alongside materials with little or no value, or worse. The issue of "internet safety" has not been revisited here because this book is more to do with teaching and learning rather than ethical dilemmas and the ills of the world at large. There is a great deal of help available for this potentially big problem, probably most notably from the UK government's internet safety information service, hosted by the Becta schools section (http://schools.becta.org.uk), the independent Internet Safety Foundation (www.isf.org.uk/) and the Get Safe Online site (www.getsafeonline.org/).

Another intention of the book is to bring to life elements of learning and pedagogical theory in the context of planned internet use and also to analyse the intentions of the teachers involved and assess the value that may have been added in the move towards accomplishing learning objectives by using an internet-based approach in comparison with any other.

By considering the range of different internet-mediated work exemplified in the preceding chapters it is clear to see that the internet is indeed a rich source of a great many educationally sound activities. It should be remembered that the examples here are a very small, and possibly even non-representative, sample of the whole. There is a good deal more useful and enjoyable material resident on the internet than can be looked at here. See companion website www.sagepub.co.uk/pritchard.

For the most part this book has not considered what is sometimes, mistakenly perhaps, considered to be the main "educational strength" of the internet, that is, the easy access provided to an almost immeasurable amount of information. Certainly the information found on the internet is a valuable source for teachers and learners alike, but making use of the information in an effective way requires planning and a sound pedagogical underpinning. This has not been explored in any detail here, but is considered in depth in an earlier volume. (Pritchard 2005)

If the summaries for each chapter are taken together and themes extracted it soon seems clear that constructivist and social constructivist theory has influenced the progress of the work described in all of the case studies of internet use. Even the activities designed to give the sort of solitary practice and repetition characteristic of more behaviourist theory have been used in ways that encourage reference to prior knowledge, interaction with others, and a consideration of methods used – all elements of constructivist theory. So, even in contexts that seem to be skewed towards a behaviouristic underpinning at the planning stage, the implementation and follow-up allowed for aspects of constructivist learning activity to flourish. Examples of this are the repetitive multiplication tasks on the Quia website, and possibly the "Find a place in the world" work. The mapping exercises were not wholly behaviouristic, but the fact that the teacher stressed lone working and, at first, discouraged talk, took away some of the possibilities for collaboration and discussion. We have seen that in all cases talk is either required, or if not, becomes an important element of the engagement for those working in close proximity to each other. The natural tendency to share, question, challenge and generally work in a sociable way seems always to come to the fore. The sensible teacher, unless there are overriding reasons for quiet, realises that there is a place for what is often very positive interaction between learners.

In the cases where individual work was preferred by the teacher there always seemed to be a time for discussion and sharing later. In plenary times the teachers often asked for experiences to be shared, methods to be explained, and for previous knowledge or understanding to be applied and compared. In some cases the links between particular aspects of work were highlighted by the children themselves – "This is just like in Quia" – something which teachers like and try to encourage. It seems that when involving the internet or any other computer-based work that is not shared in a whole-class situation, it is important to allow for a time to share what has been done, and to discuss as a whole group any knowledge, ideas or skills practised and developed. It also seems that some teachers do this as a matter of course.

Even when web-based activities are wholly behaviouristic in nature, or can be approached in that manner, teachers who would normally shy away from the "drill and practice" approach still choose to use them, but often in a modified form, and almost always supported by more constructivist ideas and follow-up activities.

There seems to be no mistaking the motivational power of the use of the internet. This phenomenon has been associated with computer use in general since computers were first trialled in schools as far back as 1980, and there have been studies of this effect over the years, showing a high correlation between computer use motivation and the achievement of higher standards (for example, Cox, 1997). Despite suggestions that the novelty effect of computer use might gradually disappear, in the case studies used here there seems to be evidence to the contrary. Motivation is generally high (dropping off occasionally), leading to high levels of engagement – a measure of success, and the enjoyment derived from being fully engaged and achieving some success. In the view of the teachers, motivation, novelty and interaction involved in many of the activities certainly played an important part in generating engagement, more so than non-computer activities might have been expected to. The teachers also seem to believe that internet use led to more enjoyable and effective learning.

When use is made of the communications capabilities of the internet there seems, from the experiences of the studies, to be an even higher level of motivation, especially if the communication is synchronous – happening in real time. With the video-conferenced language learning for example, the teacher reported that the class were more attentive than usual and sustained the attention for longer than she would have predicted. The receiving of messages by e-mail, even the anticipation, also seems to lead to excitement. This is perhaps, again, a little surprising when we consider that a number of the children involved had e-mail accounts of their own; even those claiming to be regular users of e-mail and chat were clearly enthused by the use of e-mail in the context of the recipe exchange example.

Many of the activities which we have looked at have had the effect of increasing the amount of autonomy taken on by many of the children. The teacher working with the decimal number problems on the "Builder Ted" pages wrote into her plans that she would be available to offer support, but despite the occasional apparent need for support she was not called upon. The children chose to look at the help and support facilities, or to talk to each other when they encountered a problem. If activities have a usable and easily accessible help and support facility, and as long as there is adult help nearby, it is a positive advantage for a busy teacher dealing with different groups of children if the children using the online activities are able to fend for themselves a little. Well designed activities do have this facility, but it must not be taken for granted that a help page will be a good enough substitute for a teacher's skill and insight. It would be poor practice to leave children to their own devices when working and even if they do not specifically request help, an efficient teacher will take an interest and perhaps use well focused questions or other interventions to check on the progress being made.

Examples included here are of particular projects or teaching that would simply not be possible without the sophistication of the internet – video-conferencing is a prime example of this. Other developments in video-conferencing allow for experts in remote settings – national museums or centres of excellence, to deliver one off lessons. In this way access to valuable human resources, as well as other inanimate artefacts, located in centres of excellence for example, becomes possible.

The internet in itself does not dictate an approach to teaching. However it does seem that the use of resources and remote activities mediated by the internet is more likely to lead towards more socially constructivist learning activities, if that is the approach that the teacher wants to adopt.

Teachers say that they have learned a lot about how children learn in "new" (to them and to the teacher) situations. The importance of talk is the prime example of this, and has been realised especially by the some teachers who had actually planned individual and quiet working conditions. It has been suggested earlier that there are of course times when quiet learning activities are required and seen as important – to encourage concentration, silent reading, times for assessment, or need for calm in the storm from time to time.

REVISITING THE CHARACTERISTICS OF CONSTRUCTIVIST LEARNING THAT MIGHT BE PRESENT IN ICT RELATED LESSONS

For each of the case studies a set of characteristics relating to constructivist learning was consulted and the planning, teaching and learning was measured against it. Some of the characteristics were present in abundance, some arose only occasionally and one, "Multiple perspectives", only once. It was noted earlier that the seeking out and use of information from the internet has not been a feature of the case studies; if it had been, then the presence of multiple perspectives would have been more noticeable, according to the nature of the work of course, and the range of sources used.

Table 6.1 **Number of times features of constructivist lessons with ICT recorded in case studies**

Features of constructivist lessons with ICT	No. of times recorded for all case studies
Multiple perspectives	1
Pupil-directed goals	6
Teachers as coaches	9
Metacognition	6
Learner control	9
Real-world activities and contexts	9
Knowledge construction	11
Sharing knowledge	11
Reference to what pupils know already	11
Problem solving	7
Explicit thinking about errors and misconceptions	7
Exploration	7
Peer-group learning	10
Alternative viewpoints offered	3
Scaffolding	11
Assessment for learning	5
Primary sources of data	5

Table 6.2 **Number of times other considerations/features recorded in case studies**

Other considerations/features	
Motivation	11
Enjoyment	11
Excitement	11
Novelty	11
Engagement	11
Development of work away from the computer	11
Evidence of learning	11

All of the case studies, no matter what the apparent underpinning theoretical position might have been (either in the view of the initial designer of the resource, or in the view of the teacher choosing to make use of it), provided the learners with features that were unmistakably constructivist, and generated motivation, enjoyment, excitement, novelty and engagement. Tables 6.1 and 6.2 show the total number of times that each feature was recorded in the case studies. [The maximum number of occurrences is 11, the number of case studies.]

These features can be ordered into a hierarchy of importance and, if asked, those in a position to offer an informed opinion would doubtless have differing opinions of the relative importance of each of them. For this reason it is difficult to provide such a list, but for the purposes of this chapter the following four features will be placed at the top of the list as being most desirable in lessons where ICT is used, and where constructivism is the primary concern of the teacher in terms of learning and pedagogy:

- knowledge construction
- sharing knowledge
- reference to what pupils know already
- scaffolding,

followed by:

- peer-group learning
- learner control
- real-world activities and contexts
- problem solving
- exploration.

These two groups do not lessen the importance of the remaining features, but are probably the most important of the whole list. Of the other features used to measure the value of the activities – motivation, enjoyment, excitement, novelty, engagement, development of work away from the computer, and evidence of learning – it is generally agreed that all are desirable in all lessons. For example, we would all want to see evidence of learning in lessons, and we would be hopeful that pupils enjoyed what they were doing. We also know that this is not always the case.

When we look back to the first group of four features placed at the top of the list it is gratifying to see that all of the case studies included them. Obviously the degree of presence is not measured and if the actual detail is consulted it is sometimes the case that there were supporting comments to the effect that there was "a little evidence", "scaffolding was planned for but in the event none was provided" or "some" discussion (implying not very much).

The common thread running through all of the teaching reported here, apart from the use of the internet, is the use of constructivist teaching and related pedagogy. All of the case studies, including those that would actually lend themselves very well to a far more behaviouristic approach, benefit from the approaches either planned by the teacher, or which partially evolved during the course of the work.

The question, "Does the use of the infrastructure of the internet in this example extend the possibilities for learning beyond what would have been expected if the content of the lesson had been covered in a more traditional way?" has been asked for each of the case studies. In all of the ones included (and in those not included see companion website www.sagepub.co.uk/pritchard) the answer to this question is always in the affirmative. In every case the teachers, whether new to internet use or more experienced, are clear that there were learning benefits and that the use of the internet in one way or another did lead to the learning objectives being achieved in a way that at least matched other, non-internet related approaches. In many cases it is reported that the objectives were achieved in a better, more comprehensive, way as a result of the use of the internet. It must be the case that there are forms of internet use that do not lead to improved learning, but in the case studies considered here, which are not in the form of an exhaustive survey, none were found.

One teacher commented that: "If you get it right it's amazing how they (the children) respond ... even those who you wouldn't expect it from can surprise you with what they do ... what they end up producing and what they learn."

THE INTERNET'S POTENTIAL FOR CREATING RICH LEARNING ENVIRONMENTS

The internet seems to have the potential to provide effective teaching in the cases considered here. It is of course possible to teach without the use of the internet, but we have seen here that there is great potential for improving and enlivening the learning experiences of those involved. In educational literature the notion of a "rich learning environment" is often found, but there does not seem to be a clear single definition of what is meant by this, although there is a tacit understanding by most of those involved in teaching and writing about teaching. If we attempt to define the term based on what has been written and suggested by others we can then consider the potential of the internet to provide what we assume is desirable for learners, namely a rich learning environment.

Challenge, choice and space are the three elements of a rich learning environment according to Education Testing Service (ETS), a non-profit making organisation involved in the promotion of effective learning (ETS, 2006). By "space" it is meant that there is scope and flexibility within the range of activity and work carried out. All three of these elements are seen in different proportions across the case studies here. A learning environment that is designed to be interesting, appealing and also fun, is the definition offered by Tsang and McCracken (2004), and an influential report commissioned by the Department of Education and Skills states that a rich learning environment is one "… which accesses and appeals to the different ways pupils learn." (McBer, 2000)

The internet use described in this book stands up well when compared with the variety of definitions of rich learning environments with their different emphases. However, the simple addition of an internet-related activity or source of information to a lesson will not, of itself, provide the sort of learning environment described above. The creation and maintenance of supportive, exciting and enjoyable learning experiences depends critically upon the role of the teacher. Planning needs to take into account the manifold needs, interests, dispositions, learning preferences and desired learning outcomes relating to the curriculum and to the group of children in question. The nature of the tasks set and the approach to be taken by the children – reading, writing, drawing, talking, groupwork and many more – is a crucial factor in the provision of learning environments that are rich, and which lead to enjoyable and effective learning.

It does appear that by means of a variety of internet use to support learning it is possible to create rich learning environments and in this way encourage effective learning.

SUMMARY AND RECOMMENDATIONS

The internet is a rich source of information and activity that can be used to very good effect in the classroom. If lessons involving internet use are to be effective and enjoyable the following checklist will be a useful starting point for planning.

- Plan carefully – in all studies of effective teaching there is a clear link between detailed planning and preparation, and the ultimate success of the project in terms of learning. This is equally true for lessons making use of the internet – ICT must not be the cause of losing sight of this. (In relation to ICT see TTA, 1999)

- Check sources thoroughly – reputable sources are abundant, but so are the less reputable. Even if a site is approved, or from a reliable source (the National Grid for Learning; a Local Education Authority) it is still very important to consider the content, and to make decisions concerning whether or not the activity or the information addresses the precise need that is being addressed (Chapter 2).
- Monitor carefully and support judiciously (Chapter 1).
- Build in opportunities for talking and sharing – even the most solitary or behaviouristic activities have the potential for sharing.
- In cases where lone work is expected or required consider using follow-up activities, which allow for more constructivist approaches.
- Look for opportunities to develop work away from the internet, including the use of a range of other resources (multiple perspectives).
- Encourage autonomy, but not to the point where children become "lost" in a mass of information turned up by a poorly focused search – search skills are not innate and need to be taught. In many cases, with younger children for example, it is probably best to direct learners to specific sites in order to concentrate on content rather than on searching, which can take up an inordinate amount of time and in some cases lead up many blind alleys. This in itself can be a valuable lesson but is prone to detract from the learning objectives for specific lessons.
- Do not let the technology take over your teaching. If there is a better way of achieving learning objectives that does not involve the use of the internet then it should be used. "Thinking about the use of computers in education does not mean thinking about computers. It means thinking about education." (Ellis, 1974)

Many of the points above apply equally in situations where the use of the internet does not feature. Good practice in teaching can apply across the board and to make the best use of the internet in teaching it is important not to lose sight of the principles that have been developed over the years by effective teachers, and others. It is important that sense and reason is not lost simply because of access to a new and potentially valuable technological development. Care must be taken that Daniel Chandler's words are not born out when he suggests that: "The microcomputer is a tool of awesome potency which is making it possible for educational practice to take a giant step backwards." (Chandler, 1984) The internet cannot take over from good teaching and good teaching is focused on the needs of the learners and on clear learning objectives – not on resources for learning, which follow on from this starting point, not lead the way.

Appendices

APPENDIX 1   PEDAGOGICAL AND THEORETICAL CONSIDERATIONS: EXPLANATORY NOTES

Characteristics of constructivist learning that might be present in ICT: Questions to consider	
Multiple perspectives	Were different viewpoints offered by the website or other resources?
Pupil-directed goals	Did children decide their own goals or courses of action?
Teachers as coaches	Were the teachers involved teaching in terms of telling the children certain things, or guiding them towards finding out?
Metacognition	Is there any specifically metacognitive activity encouraged; is there any as an unintended result?
Learner control	Do the children have a degree of control over what they are doing and how they go about it? Are they able to make decisions about the progress of what they are doing?
Real-world activities and contexts	Is the work set in a "real" or mainly authentic context?
Knowledge construction	Is opportunity to actively construct new knowledge provided? (c.f. practice and revision).
Sharing knowledge	Are there opportunities to share new knowledge and understanding with others?
Reference to what pupils know already	Is existing prior knowledge activated and referred to at the outset and during the work?
Problem solving	Are children involved in problem solving activities?
Explicit thinking about errors and misconceptions	Are errors and misconceptions highlighted and made the focus of development?
Exploration	Are opportunities for exploring the topic and associated contiguous areas provided?

Peer-group learning	Are opportunities provided for peer–peer interactions, activity and decision making?
Alternative viewpoints offered	Are the children provided with alternative opinions or viewpoints concerning issues that may be controversial?
Scaffolding	Is appropriate support provided in a number of different ways – adult intervention, alternative activities, amended resources, and so on?
Assessment for learning	Is there opportunity for teachers to make assessments which will inform the next stages of learning?
Primary sources of data	Are children involved with the use of first hand data sources?

Other considerations/features	
Motivation	Does the activity seem to act as a motivational factor, including the motivation often offered by computer/internet use?
Enjoyment	Do the children seem to enjoy what they are doing?
Excitement	Does the work or the prospect of the work engender excitement?
Novelty	Is there any novelty effect, either in the nature of the activity, or simply in the use of the computer/internet?
Engagement	Is there a good level of engagement with the activities?
Development of work away from the computer	Does the work "at" the computer lead to development and other related activity away from the computer?
Evidence of learning	What evidence is there of learning having taken place?

APPENDIX 2   CASE STUDIES

	Title	Focus	Location(s)
	Chapter 3: Working individually		
3.1	Drilling for tables	Practice and revision	www.quia.com
3.2	Builder Ted and decimals	Practice and revision	www.bbc.co.uk/education/mathsfile/ shockwave/games/laddergame.html
3.3	Find a place in the world	Learning facts	www.mape.org.uk/startower/world/resources/ broken.htm www.nwlg.org/pages/-resources/mapgames/ geog.html www.amblesideprimary.com/ambleweb/clickon/ index.htmLabel www.mape.org.uk/startower/world/index.htm
	Chapter 4: Working collaboratively		
4.1	Virtual tour of the Cabinet War Rooms	Exploration and investigation	http://cwr.iwm.org.uk/
4.2	Exploring places of worship	Exploration and investigation	www.hitchams.suffolk.sch.uk/synagogue/ index.htm
4.3	Key stage 1 music games	Learning facts and skills	www.bbc.co.uk/northernireland/schools/ 4_11/music/mm/index.shtml

	Title	Focus	Location(s)
	Chapter 5: Longer term projects, communicating and problem solving		
5.1	Key stage 1 health education	Exploration and learning	http://www.welltown.gov.uk/ www.wiredforhealth.gov.uk/ http://www.rope-skipping.be/ http://www.saskschools.ca/~gregory/gym/skiptips.html
5.2	Modern foreign languages and video-conferencing	Language learning	http://www.global-leap.com/ http://www.globalgateway.org.uk
5.3	Children publishing their work: Sports day on the internet	Journalism; writing for an audience	
5.4	International recipe exchange via e-mail	Communicating	http://www.global-leap.com/
5.5	Using a webquest	Investigating a topic	www.webquestuk.org.uk/

References

Alexander, R. (1992) *Policy and Practice in Primary Education*. London: Routledge.

Bartlett, F.C. (1958) *Thinking*. New York: Basic Books.

BBC (2002) *Maths File Game Show*: http://www.bbc.co.uk/education/mathsfile/shockwave/games/laddergame.html (Accessed 27.10.06)

BBC (undated) *Musical Mysteries for Key Stages 1 and 2*. BBC Northern Ireland: www.bbc.co.uk/northernireland/schools/4_11/music/mm/index.shtml (Accessed 27.10.06)

BBC (undated) *Children of World War Two*: www.bbc.co.uk/history/ww2children/ (Accessed 22.07.06)

British Council (2006) *Global Gateway*: www.globalgateway.org.uk/ (Accessed 29.09.06)

Brown, A. (1987) Metacognition, executive control, self-regulation and other more mysterious mechanisms. In F.E. Weinert, and R.H. Kluwe (eds) *Metacognition, Motivation and Understanding* 65–116. Laurence Erlbaum: Mahwah, NJ.

Brown, J. S., Collins, A. and Duguid, P. (1989) 'Situated cognition and the culture of learning', *Educational Researcher,* 18 (1) 32–42.

Bruner, J. (1996) *The Culture of Education*. Cambridge, MA: Harvard University Press.

Central Advisory Council for Education (CACE) (1967) *Children and their Primary Schools* (The Plowden Report). London: HMSO.

Chandler, D. (1984) *Young Learners and the Microcomputer*. Milton Keynes: Open University Press.

Chastain, K. (1971) *The Development of Modern Language Skills: Theory to Practice*. Philadelphia: Center for Curriculum Development.

Cordes, C. and Miller, E. (2000) *Fool's Gold: A Critical Look at Computers in Childhood*. College Park, MD: Alliance for Childhood.

Cox, M. (1997) *Impact of Information Technology on Student's Motivation: Final Report*. London: King's College.

CWR (undated) *Cabinet War Rooms and Churchill Museum*: http://cwr.iwm.org.uk/ (Accessed 15.07.06)

Department for Education and Employment (DfEE) Qualifications and Curriculum Authority (QCA) (1999) *The National Curriculum*. London: DFEE/QCA.

(DES) (1982) *Mathematics Counts* (Cockcroft Report). London: HMSO.

Department for Education and Skills (DfES) (1998) *Circular number 4/98 Annex B: Initial Teacher Training Curriculum for the Use of Information and Communications Technology in Subject Teaching*. London: DfES. www.dfes.gov.uk/publications/guidanceonthelaw/ 4_98/annexb.htm (Accessed 30.05.06)

Department for Education and Skills (DfES) (2004a) www.becta.org.uk/page_documents/research/ict_in_schools_survey_2004.pdf

Department for Education and Skills (DfES) (2004b) *Pedagogy and Practice. Creating Effective Learners: Using ICT to Enhance Learning*. London: DfES. Also available at: www.standards.dfes.gov.uk/keystage3/downloads/sec_pptl043804u15using_ict.pdf (Accessed 06.11.06)

Department for Education and Skills (DfES) (undated) *Super Highway Safety*: http://stage-safety.ngfl.gov.uk/schools/ (Accessed 14.01.06)

Department for Education and Skils (DfES) (undated) *ICT at Key Stages 1 and 2: Unit 6A. Multimedia Presentation*: www.standards.dfes.gov.uk/schemes2/it/itx6a/ (Accessed 12.12.05)

Department of Education and Skills (DfES) Department of Health (DoH) (2004) *Welltown*: www.welltown.gov.uk/ (Accessed 20.10.06)

Department for Education and Skills (DfES) Qualifications and Curriculum Authority (QCA) (1997–2006) *The Standards Site: Schemes of Work*: www.standards.dfes.gov.uk/schemes3/ (Accessed 17.10.06)

Department of Health (DOH) (undated) *Wired for Health: helping schools become healthy and effective*: www.wiredforhealth.gov.uk/ (Accessed 20.10.06)

Dern, D.P. (1994) *The Internet Guide for New Users*. Maidenhead: McGraw-Hill.

Dickens, C. (1981) *Hard Times* Chapman and Hall: London.

Dodge, B. (1997) *Some Thoughts About WebQuests*: http://webquest.sdsu.edu/about_webquests. html (Accessed 16.10.05)

Ellis, A. (1974) *The Use and Misuses of Computers*. New York: McGraw-Hill.

Education Testing Service (ETS) (2006) *Brain Compatible Learning Environments*: www.ets.org (Accessed 16.11.06)

European Schoolnet (undated) *Pedagogical FAQ*: www.eun.org/eun.org2/eun/en/print_ preview.cfm?oid=856 (Accessed 29.05.06)

Fennema, E. and Franke, M.L. (1992) "Teachers' Knowledge and its Impact', in Grouws, D.A. (Ed.), *Handbook of Research on Mathematics Teaching and Learning*": 147–64. New York: Macmillan Publishing Company.

Fisher, E. (1996) "Distinctive features of pupil–pupil classroom talk and their relationship to learning: How discursive exploration might be encouraged". *Language and Education*, 7, 239–257.

Flavell, J.H. (1976) "Metacognitive Aspects of Problem Solving", in Resnick (Ed.) *The Nature of Intelligence*, (pp. 231–235). New Jersey: Lawrence Erlbaum Associates.

Flavell, J.H. (1977) *Cognitive Development*. New Jersey: Prentice-Hall.

Furr, G.C. (2003) "'Paperless Classroom' to 'Deep Reading': Five Stages in Internet Pedagogy" in *The Technology Source Archives*, originally published in *The Technology Source* (http://ts.mivu.org/) as Grover C. Furr III "From 'Paperless Classroom' to 'Deep Reading': Five Stages in Internet Pedagogy". http://technologysource.org/article/from_paperless_class-room_to_deep_reading/ (Accessed 6.11.06)

Gage, N. (1985) *Hard Gains in the Soft Sciences: The Case for Pedagogy* CEDR Monograph Bloomington: Phi Delta Kappa.

Galton, M. (200) Integrating Theory and Practice: Teachers' Perspectives on Educational Research. Paper given in parallel session of the first TLRP conference 9–10 November 2000).

Gardner, H. (1993) *Multiple Intelligences: The theory in practice*. New York: Basic Books.

Hammond, M. (2004) "The Peculiarities of Teaching Information and Communication Technology as a Subject: A Study of Trainee and New ICT Teachers in Secondary Schools", *Technology, Pedagogy and Education*, 13 (1) 29–42.

Hitchams (2006) *Synagogues*: www.hitchams.suffolk.sch.uk/synagogue/index.htm (Accessed 20.10.06)

Holland, J.H., Holyoak, K.J., Nisbett, R.E. and Thagard, P.R. (1986) *Induction: Processes of Inference, Learning and Discovery*. Cambridge, MA: MIT Press.

Johnson-Laird, P. (1983) *Mental Models: Towards a Cognitive Science of Language, Inference, and Consciousness*. Cambridge (USA): Harvard University Press.

Jonassen, D.H., Peck, K.L, and Wilson, B.G. (1999) *Learning with Technology: A constructivistic perspective*. Upper Saddle River, NJ: Prentice Hall, Inc.

Lave, J. and Wenger, E. (1991) *Situated Learning*. CUP: Cambridge.

Lewisham (undated) "Back to the playground': *The website that gives information about Skipping Rhymes And Playtime Games*": http://ecs.lewisham.gov.uk/youthspace/ca/Rosieskip/skippin-gone.htm (Accessed 12.11.06)

McBer, H. (2000) *Research into Teacher Effectiveness: A Model of Teacher Effectiveness Report to the Department for Education and Employment*. London: DfEE.

Mayer, R.E. (1983) *Thinking: Problem Solving and Cognition*. New York: W. H. Freeman & Co.

Mercer, N. (1994) "The quality of talk in children's joint activity at the computer", *Journal of Computer Assisted Learning*, 10, 24–32.

Mortimore, P. (1999) *Understanding Pedagogy and Its Impact on Learning*. Paul Chapman: London.

Mosely, J. (1998) *Quality Circle Time in the Primary Classroom: Your Essential Guide to Enhancing Self-Esteem, Self-Discipline and Positive Relationships*. Cambridge: LDA.

National Statistics (2006) *Office for National Statistics*: www.statistics.gov.uk/cci/nugget.asp?id=8 (Accessed 24.09.06)

NC Online (undated) Access to the Non-Statutory National Framework for RE: www.nc.uk.net/webdav/servlet/XRM (Accessed 14.07.06)

North Central Regional Educational Laboratory (NCREL) (1996) *Plugging In: Choosing and Using Educational Technology*: www.ncrel.org/

North Central Regional Educational Laboratory (NCREL) (undated) *New Times Demand New Ways of Learning* http://www.ncrel.org/ (Accessed 06.06.05)

Phillips, T. (1990) "Structuring context for exploratory talk", in D. Wray (Ed.), *Talking and Listening* (pp. 60–72). Leamington Spa: Scholastic.

Piaget, J. and Inhelder, B. (1969) *The Psychology of the Child*. New York: Basic Books.

Pritchard, A. (2005) *Learning on the Net: A Practical Guide to Enhancing Learning in Primary Classrooms*. London: David Fulton.

QCA (1999) *The National Curriculum*: www.nc.uk.net/ (Accessed 10.10.06)

QCA (1999) *The National Curriculum for Design and Technology* (Programme of Study for Key Stage 2) London: QCA. Also at www.nc.uk.net/ (Accessed 11.10.06)

QCA (1997–2006) *RE at key stages 1 and 2* (Year 1) Unit 1F: *What can we learn from visiting a church?*: www.standards.dfes.gov.uk/schemes2/religion/rel1f/

QCA (undated) *History at key stages 1 and 2 Unit 9: What Was it Like for Children in the Second World War?*: www.standards.dfes.gov.uk/schemes2/history/his9/?view=get (Accessed 17.7.06)

Quia (2006) www.quia.com (Accessed 21.09.06)

Reynolds, D. (1998) "Teacher Effectiveness", Presentation at the Teacher Training Agency Corporate Plan Launch 1998–2001. London: TTA.

Rodrigues, S. (1997) 'Fitness for Purpose: a glimpse at where, why and how to use information technology in science lessons', *Australian Science Teachers Journal*, 43 (2) 33–9.

Rumelhart, D.E. and Norman, D.A. (1976). *Accretion, turning and restructuring: three modes of learning*. (Report no. 7602).(ERIC Document Reproduction Service No. ED134902).

Schank, R.C. (1975) *Conceptual Information Processing*. New York: Elsevier.

Selinger, M. (2001) "*Setting Authentic Tasks Using the Internet* in Leask, M. (ed.) (2001) *Issues in Teaching Using ICT*" (96–104). London: Routledge Falmer.

Sewell, D. (1990) *New tools for New Minds*. Harvester Wheatsheaf: London.

Simon, B. (1994) *The State and Educational Change: Essays in the HIstory of Education of Pedagogy*. London: Lawrence & Wishart.

Somekh, B. (2000) "New technology and learning: policy and practice in the UK, 1980–2010", *Journal of Education and Information Technologies*, 5 (1): 19–37

Tsang, H. and McCracken, J. (2004) *The Role for Rich Multimedia Learning* Proceeding of Computers and Advanced Technology in Education (CATE) Kauai, Hawaii. Available at: www.actapress.com/PDFViewer.aspx?paperId=17053 (Accessed 12.11.06)

TTA (1999) *Ways Forward with ICT: Effective Pedagogy using Information and Communications Technology in Literacy and Numeracy in Primary Schools*. London: TTA.

Varian, H. (undated) www.kincumber.com/howbig.htm (Accessed 08.11.06) (University of California at Berkeley).

"Webb, M.E. (2002) 'Pedagogical Reasoning: Issues and Solutions for the Teaching and Learning of ICT in Secondary Schools", *Education and Information Technologies*, 7 (3) 237–55.

Webquest UK (undated) www.webquestuk.org.uk/ (Accessed 16.10.03)

Woods, P. (1996) *Researching the Art of Teaching: ethnography for educational use*. London: Routledge.

Index